Praise for *Look at This Blue*

"Here is a lifetime, relentless, inviting us bravely to sit in a circle facing the fire, speaking. Allison's new collection covers her poetic depth and practice: travels, research, vision and visions, her wide wingspan—saving the people, the planet, and creatures. It is timely as all her books have been through the decades. Yet, the approach is radical, experimental. She meditates and dances through the trails of the text. Love and suffering, document and lyrical flight, human core and cosmic interrelationship, woman's body and explosive mind. A prizewinner all the way. A warm, true heart."
—Juan Felipe Herrera

"Song from both above and within a texture of bad change, imbued with beauty, being in and of nature. This language, these careful lines, implicates us all as bits of process of extinction, violent—humans, together with the Xerces blue butterfly and California's so many other spectacular species, lovingly named. Voices, vegetation, animals, human recall and event, like scratchings or petroglyphs. Who's speaking? The record. A gorgeous, scary poem."
—Alice Notley

"Both ode and elegy for our natural and man-made environments, Allison Hedge Coke's *Look at This Blue* speaks of California's inevitable loss, its 'temporal melt,' its 'death-wish façade.' Hedge Coke calligraphies this tragedy and mythos with such poignance that you will be riveted until the collection's very last line. *Look at This Blue* is not only timely; it is necessary."
—Lynne Thompson

"How blue are you? Xerces-butterfly blue, coyote-eye blue, lake blue, Mission blue: this is the blue of beauty and the blue of grief. *Look at This Blue* is a necessary reckoning with the ongoing, disastrous, criminal genocide perpetuated in the Golden State, amongst the beauty and riches of its landscape. As Hedge Coke writes, the poem is 'the offering we make.'"
—Eleni Sikelianos

"Allison Adelle Hedge Coke sings California with a garden of images, all life, named and splendidly watered by bewitching words—but this is no romantic paean. She documents genocide, massacres, slavery, arsons, lies, the laments of the pushed out and knocked down. Here's the hardest truth, wrapped in lyric."   **—Luis J. Rodríguez**

"Allison Adelle Hedge Coke's *Look at This Blue* is a song for California: a poem as big, as diverse, as ambitious as the state it celebrates. Or do I mean the state it eulogizes? Or do I mean the state whose histories it sets straight? Or do I mean the state this poem seeks to save? Or do I mean the state of the poet whose story is part and parcel of the story of this same state in all its grim and glorious broken beauty? Yes, I mean these things and more. Much more. This is a poem whose borders extend beyond geography and territory and history. This is a poem to be lived."

—Dean Rader

"Allison Adelle Hedge Coke is one of the most important and innovative environmental writers of our time. *Look at This Blue* urgently asks us to see the wondrous biodiversity of the planet amidst the violent ravages of colonialism, capitalism, and ecological imperialism. Throughout, this cyclical poem sows dreams of a 'bettering world' where our relationships with the earth and more-than-human species are replenished through justice, protection, and love."   **—Craig Santos Perez**

"From Ishi to Riverside fairy shrimp, from sandhill cranes to vast human damage, Allison Adelle Hedge Coke calls out and calls to California in *Look at This Blue*. The book is a poem is a list, naming the eighty-four who died in the Camp Fire in Paradise, the millions killed in their native landscapes and internment camps and everywhere else. It reminds us of the extinct Xerces blue butterfly and, page after page, of the endangered ones: delta smelt, riparian woodrat, Sierra Nevada yellow-legged frog, Mono Lake diving beetle, finback whale, a list that, as it grows, becomes profound, tragic, gorgeous, overwhelming, and eventually a song. But a song not to be sung without the accompanying verses of greed and power, of politics, massacre, incarceration, exclusion. Not even the missing are missing: we are all included. The title repeats through the text as a chorus, a tow-line to hang on to, at one point referring to the chance mutation of coyote eye color, at another, the Hidden Lake bluecurl flower, fifty of which will fit on a penny. This is a book for the world we currently inhabit, the long unstoppable chaos, the season of losing everything we love. Listen. Let yourself belong. 'Recite their names now,' Hedge Coke asks us, coaxes us, dares us in her clear voice, unafraid.

And then she names an appendix of resource links: 'do the work.'"

—Molly Fisk

"Holding this book in your hand, you catch the scent of high desert salvia and a whiff of charred ancient forests. Pyrocumulus loom over this text, an assemblage in the vein of Juan Felipe Herrera and C. D. Wright, etched in chants of forewarning and loss. Hedge Coke's reckoning with the genocide of the Indigenous and the mass extinction of endemic species bares the roots of conflagration throughout 'Indian Country, California, every bit.' *Look at This Blue* is itself a blue flame that comes to us in time."

—Sesshu Foster

"*Look at This Blue* is a fiercely pulsating journey of love and despair. The earth crackles, the body heaves in these wrenching snapshots of personal, historical, and environmental disasters. You want to look away, but you can't, as Allison Hedge Coke chronicles all the ways we are broken, our bone-deep griefs. Above and beneath these losses, she offers us singular joys: the trill of sandhill cranes, a girl with 'eyes the green of August,' small porpoises that 'undulate in air.' A list of resources at the end urges us toward the work of survival. We are still on the hook." **—Diana García**

"In *Look at This Blue*, Allison Hedge Coke pulls us into a meditation on the entangled history of California's ecological and racial catastrophes, which shape the place's past and present. In an unapologetic disquisition focused on the actualities of California's Indigenous peoples and their land, Hedge Coke lays bare the course that made way to the burning, flooding, splintering realities that shape California today. Both astonishing and piercing, hopeful and solemn, *Look at This Blue* plunges the reader into the fractal distortion of seeing the sun from underneath the water. This is a poem of urgency, of sorrow and memory, a call for us to see anew and change the destructive path we're on before we are all consumed by it." **—Matthew Shenoda**

"What Hedge Coke provides readers in the pages that follow is the lightning rod. Her long poem slips in and out of images of violence against the land, specifically California, the flora and fauna and many immigrants and Indigenous peoples of that land, the poor and cast out and overlooked and neglected and abused of that land, ever aware of the undercurrents that connect each transgression. While I've grown suspicious that one can give voice to the voiceless without doing further violence, these lines are not acts of ventriloquism, nor even quiet moments of witnessing. These are the aftershocks of the violences we as a nation would not see, haunting the periphery until there is nowhere we can look without being made at last to see. But in this litany of those who have been lost and those who are at risk, so too there is an act of preservation, a summons, and offering. If not promise, then a charge, a spark, to move us along. This book is like nothing I've seen from Hedge Coke before. It was just what I needed to read right now." **—Abigail Chabitnoy, *Orion Magazine***

LOOK AT THIS BLUE

Also by Allison Adelle Hedge Coke

Dog Road Woman
Off-Season City Pipe
Streaming
Blood Run
Burn
The Year of the Rat
Rock, Ghost, Willow, Deer

LOOK AT THIS BLUE

A Poem

Allison Adelle Hedge Coke

COFFEE HOUSE PRESS

Minneapolis
2022

Coffee House Press books are available to the trade through our primary distributor, Consortium Book Sales & Distribution, cbsd.com or (800) 283-3572. For personal orders, catalogs, or other information, write to info@coffeehousepress.org.

Coffee House Press is a nonprofit literary publishing house. Support from private foundations, corporate giving programs, government programs, and generous individuals helps make the publication of our books possible. We gratefully acknowledge their support in detail in the back of this book.

Excerpts have been previously published in *Cordite*, *Walt's Corner/ Long Islander News*, *AWP Writers Chronicle*, *Ploughshares*, an anthology for *Playa*, and a *Poetry & Science* group poet chapbook by Scarlet Tanager Books.

LIBRARY OF CONGRESS CATALOGING-IN-PUBLICATION DATA

Names: Hedge Coke, Allison Adelle, author.
Title: Look at this blue : a poem / Allison Adelle Hedge Coke.
Identifiers: LCCN 2021053386 (print) | LCCN 2021053387 (ebook) |
    ISBN 9781566896207 (paperback) | ISBN 9781566896290 (epub)
Subjects: LCGFT: Poetry.
Classification: LCC PS3553.O4366 L66 2022 (print) |
    LCC PS3553.O4366 (ebook) | DDC 811/.54—dc23/eng/20211029
LC record available at https://lccn.loc.gov/2021053386
LC ebook record available at https://lccn.loc.gov/2021053387

PRINTED IN THE UNITED STATES OF AMERICA
30 29 28 27 26 25 24 23   2 3 4 5 6 7 8 9

Look at This Blue

for my blue butterfly, Hazel Brianne

for Marija, Diana & Paul,
for the quiet rooms

for California, our beloved

once, the world was gleaming, open, we entered
unknowing, believing all we came to
we must deserve, knowing we did not   faced
extinction

"*The path we have taken has rotted*
Ignite, stand upright, conduct yourself like lightning"

—Tanya Tagaq, "Retribution"

an assemblage

LOOK AT THIS BLUE

Look at This Blue

Xerces blue butterfly   *from the sand dunes of San Francisco*
      first-known American butterfly to become extinct due to humans
      first known

Redwood burls cut like blisters shaved from trunks
                              poach life source from root
killing giants in knobby growth removals
                              baseline / canopy-height bud tissue
unsprouted genetic code for clone of parent-tree emergence—

Barrel at my mouth, ready-cocked   held there
                              by my baby brother's bared grip.

Lemon-wedge half-moon pops over
                    flat Cosumnes shallows
over sweet sound, low rustle in Lodi water
                    chortle trill night language from standing
cranes, sandhills, they've been there
                    all along, standing still knee-deep in station pools.

          Orion hovering eastward   drawn, readied.
Someone slinks past doorjamb
          each choke hold felled   vaporizes   cognizance.

In a world fast shaking herself loose

from diabolical torrent.

Rising throttle song above throttled breath

choked out between calligraphies,

madness clenched   fury   unfurled release

misery met in each pummeled break

it's not over.

Sleep in despair   sleeping moth-tongue, unrolled against central incisors,

human-throated,   deep yearns for saxophone

trachea   windpipe—

Sandhills chortle only saving grace   wetlands marshalled.

Nothing here on guardian watch.

Riverside.
Reaching back for slipped skateboard
                          he was hit so hard he flew while breaking.

A crow above, whose wings were sunning, swooped
                          at the same time the car careened to halt
on Martin Luther King Road

near Bordwell Park, Eastside, where the speed limit suddenly increases
while approaching two close crosswalks leading to homes from Stratton
Community Center, Bordwell, Emerson Elementary—Eastside; Black,
brown kids; elders—
                          Anyone can see someone once worked this out.

Ishi *died thirteen years before I was born,*
                    so I have no nice anecdotes about knowing
him when I was a child. I'm sorry.
                                —Ursula K. Le Guin

It was custom to be introduced by name, not to utter own. UC Berkeley chose
man/Ishi for a name for him, which he (accepted).

He worked as a research assistant in the anthropology department.
He was placed into a museum in the anthropology department.

      Yana continued living in California.

      After declaration that Ishi
    was the last of his people, at least
    four other Yahi were seen in the
    bush.

Yana [was] an agglutinative, polysynthetic
language with SVO word order. The Yana
language was distinctive in having different
word forms used by male and female speakers,
an unusual trait that does not exist in the other
languages of this region.

      1999, Ishi's brain returned to Yana people, his closest relatives

"It's all going to burn," says man accused of setting Holy Fire

First the puma in Santa Paula palm branch, then coyotes, fox, rabbits
appear, birds overcome sky   plume,
                    then the entire yard a carpet of undulating fleas
so thick wrapping that bread bags over feet and ankles
                    barely made it passable.
Everything escaping heat from fire-stormed arson   120,000 acres
                    blanket-fired Los Padres National Forest and more

                    choking like the child they found, still hung—

Sleep in the dream of bettering world.
                    Sleep in the dream/nightmare woken.

What we carry howls   boggling
                    her cheek contorts in flame unfanned   yet fanning.

She eclipses all asunder, all broken.
                    Scar face vision in temporal melt.

Somewhere on my left face, you can still see
                    where it was sewn back on.

On the right, the line across eyelid
                    where it was sewn back on.
          On the abdomen the line
                    where it was sewn back, sewn back, sewn back.
Somewhere on my right hand
                    where it was sewn.

          All the heres and theres
                    where sewn.

All the labia biopsies, removals, explorations,   assaults, sewn.

          1985–2000.   1963–1996.

What we carry weeps   wet-haired
                    her cheek contorts when sprayed by guard.

                    From the first time she attempted, her neck ached.

Meanwhile, here, a third body in Baldwin Hills fire, more missing
                                                    arson again
          someone   *is out there.*

Look at This Blue

Palos Verdes blue   from the Palos Verdes Peninsula
            one of the best claims to being world's rarest butterfly
            first thought extinct by development
rediscovered by Rick Rogers, Rudi Mattoni, and Timothy Dahlum
                    at the Defense Fuel Support Point in San Pedro

            newly returned lays eggs on deerweed
notice the patterning on the underside of wing

Child choked out, belt at throat.

               She returned to me in dreams.

Child choked out, belt at throat.

               She returned to me in dreams.

Child choked out, belt at throat.

               She returned to me in dreams.

Child choked out, belt at throat.

               She returned to me in dreams.

Child choked out, belt at throat.

               She returned to me in dreams.

Child choked out, belt at throat.

               She returned to me in dreams.

Child choked out, belt at throat.

               She returned to me in dreams.

Child choked out, belt at throat.

               She returned to me in dreams.

They were only there seeking psychiatric help.

She'd been exceptionally mean for days

Their grandson rode along while they sorted what they could of it, while her

schizophrenia played out all sorts.

They turned into the intersection by the mall in Ventura
a big tank of a thing T-boned them
right down the middle of the car.
So concussed, cops gave their ATM PIN to taxi home.

He'd lost a tooth. Grandson's nose broken.
She broke a leg. All three concussed.
The dog in the other car was dizzy, some say.

Later, she took a call from her son, headed out to wire away her war widow's
pension.

Walking on an unattended broken leg.   Senior living.

Remember, along the way, the murdered sow bear, her cubs taken for claws.

We're all just symptoms of something massive faster over

they're killing us.
weaponizing nature, sanctifying arms, consecrating each trigger-flexed
hand.

Dad, in his eighties, on the trailer roof sprayer in hand fighting back
ignition

not leaving until everyone leaves,
or the time he battled out of being rolled,   just smoothly
turned his cane horizontal,
asking punks who should join him when he dies, soon enough,
until they scramble
cross K-Mart parking lot.

Trigger turned to face, every right to bear bitter, every night-schemed
daybreak flash
no need to fictionalize this dude
is what he is, what man made, what man.

Sliced labia squamous,   first
                             somewhere midtwenties.

                                    Missing children, women, taken
            somewhere.
            For me it was a gulley, a pond, a base, a van, a hall, a window—

Here, where her hair shone blue-black all over her time.
             Where, throughout our childhood, we never cherished it.
Yet when found on others, we loved them, coveted
             long, horselike tails our lovers threw over their
shoulders, our own blue-black love we needed to know, never felt,
             until the later years when we couldn't get enough of her.

             What was wronged there, woven?
             What bind was pulled when dog stole soup?

Blankets, Pendletons, all blue as well, some with black
             some with red, yellow to bring sun
into this longing place, this place of loss, longing.

             Throughout childhood, we never cherished it.
In her pyre, we gathered all of these with her, let it smolder   loved.

INS showed up morning sometime

        after he demanded IRS pay him back-owed arrears.

"When were you last in Mexico?" they asked his wife.

        Our honeymoon, 1950. "When will you return to
        Mexico?"

        they

           ask.

We're too old to travel, they note.

        His call came late. Where are your mother's

naturalization papers? Her green card. Can you fax them

        to INS, to IRS? They put your mother in a van to deport

to Mexico. She's Canadian, you note. Black hair, black eyes,

        short, dark complexioned, Mexican enough, he says.

SB-622 Civil Detention Facilities: State Investigation.

        Within 90 days after the individual's death,

the Department of Justice shall make a public report

        Could be any mama.

Once a flat

flat

shell

brain husk
        with no dendrite,
            no axon, no crystalline mass
branch impulse at synapse
            no hope within husks of men, self-molded
set to burgeon, fixate boulders,
            once marbled giant, now fixed flat
to hurl, catapult incendiary, tension-
            launching slingshot (de)vice *Tweet*

        Let it be an arms race,
        we will outmatch them
        at every pass and outlast
            them all.   Any them,
                at all.

                Then it was
            done, or almost so.

State mirrors cried:

beautiful boy,

                     made to eat cat feces,
vomit, pepper sprayed, made
                    to live in a cabinet, box,
bound and gagged at eight because you might be gay.

             Beautiful child taken at ten, beaten, tortured,
Malnourished; whose mother, father
             tore into, pummeled for coming out,
for coming out.

California's largest utility could face murder charges . . .

if found responsible for sparking recent, deadly wildfires

around the state

Daily Caller

PG&E pleads guilty to 84 counts of involuntary manslaughter over Camp fire

LA Times

Equations made to name propensities, longing, departures,
intrusion, infusions, all as one needs
to be viable in the state or lack thereof.

Where man goes, comes inevitable loss, it was
always this way, intrusion, infusions, all as one needs.

After tens of thousands of generations, now
lain a mile or so deep under grounds long overwashed
in a world gone awry, the
remains of the day buried by the flow and ebb to it.
This morning 185 mph winds wind.

          Where fish caches still lie, untouched and
frozen beneath our own remains, introspective delights,
                    egomanias,   here they lie
awaiting rebirths into sparks of life above
                    even still untouched, cold there. Waiting
for fires to bear life, carbons still, like embers, cold yet.

Here, we once knew balance, achieved it, lived it.
                              Any one of them left to themselves if they
                              maneuvered away
from agreement reached with all of the natural   world.
                              Where only one of the many
now overthrown and imbalanced
                              by intrusion by who left ideology of
balance for warscapes, resourcing, in a way
                              tangled to harness everything met.

                              In some discovery mode and taking, it never
                              ended, still goes on and now
even rainwater for sale so harnessed
                              for commodity,   for resource in a green
time now long-over, browned in drought made
                              by sourcing rain givers, savanna grasses,
forests, sea oats in a time where everything is
                              commodified,   so taken
to other places now without, in this time
                              of no ways to meander in a
continual manner, now, everything must
                              shift, we will surely not endure, stones sigh.

There is not joy in it and man is now the antibiosis
                         symbiotic relation
shared with all completely unearthed
                         scathed, hotter, only those
who see past retain understanding
                         time, place, safety   give back
to keep balance sure, a timely whole
                         equal, many trees
canopy, rain,
                         give life again to the spark of energy necessary
to star starwood reborn again
                         lifting lights on deserts over
geological spots giving spherical visitations.

We need balance. Need keep from
what may kill us all   what may
                    end us.   Distinguish an atom, a
gathered molecule, something we must
                    in each and every touch in this life in
every single moment of solitude and in
                    silence in the coming and going of River and her
embodiment of so many other beings she
                    nurtures to replenish us with the life givers the
fish she bears and birds who seek her
                    for snails and protection as we seek River for
healing to rekindle us in our own winterings.
                    Now is the time to return to what we do with
our partnerships in life, the cranes impressing
                    us for generation upon generation giving us
dances and life and reason and approach to
                    enjoy the reason we were gifted these particular atoms.

To stone walls, to everything residual here
                         languages morph
balance   standing on one leg and the other,
                       jet forward leap, crane dance
all balance and reason understood every motive
                       or deference, rearing young
conditioning note, absolute calling for more
                       rain all around in beauty bringing
snail to surface keeping predator under cover
                       searching for mouse rather than bird prey.

Shell-shocked. Gullied.

After he cut this hand, severed tendon,
                    punched this face, mocked,
                    bruised, cut—punched again—
his Ventura County public defender, a woman,
                    asked me to drop charges so he
wouldn't miss class.
                         Not happening.
                         Not happening.
                         Not happening.
Guilty; she won Suspended Imp anyway.
                    This is how roadside trash pick-up equates even.

Broken branch in canopy, trees, like fingers, like stiff blade through my
right hand,
                         bone handle separating knuckles
like gales tearing muscle bearing my keen weight.

                      Or E. coli.
Some salad in the back aisle,
                        invader, like this guy.

Too idiotic to merit note, past criminal code
                        when pressing limits, cruelties

as method of stopping poems so
                        they could not escape

no matter the muse-scape. Santa Anas, floods, frost on orange grove—

All that counted elsewise,
                        was any snowfall on Topatopa

something lost on death-wish facade
                        calling itself *man.*

Ghost knocks pounded behind my head on the wall
                        when he tried to stay here.

Enigma, can we still use this?

        Maybe we are, I am.

Not in the way Lopez would

        call *Bruja* when plant hangers split,

oranges flew, unaided.

        Chairs bobbed like mergansers in quakes.

Northridge, maybe wildest

        we'd met. Pipe bomb, some believed.

In the still no one questioned

        some thrilled by variance, by her shaking us loose.

Behind us Limoneira, a town of a camp
                 now some suburbia development,
then all sorts of workers, growers, since 1893,
Rancho Sespe, Flores y Cantos, la Lucha we would go—
                 Santa Paula, Fillmore, Piru
Oxnard strawberries, Saticoy records, Ventura gold beaches
                 hot peppers shouldering Blood Alley Ventura Freeway, 126
oleanders, eucalyptus, rhododendron.
                 I came from the camps. Not these, but I served these
children. Decades ago, one Olivelands seven-year-old
                 girl wrote,
                 my eyes are the green of August.
I still see her eyes, her August, now.

Condors replenish.   Phoenix, half-grown chick, survived Big Sur fire, matured,

fathered egg with Redwood Queen,
                    whose initial mate was lost to Dolan fire
                    all phoenix rise
                    blue-green egg until milky, milky way split
open up in some hollowed redwood, on cave floor dust, cliff edge

Once, my hand gleaned plume from cliff edge
                    something called me to reach in, feel
what left it gone   fingers rake pulled from pit
                    what remnant left there.

Left there.

Let love lead.

Let hand that pummeled rest.

Let scowl rest, face relieve.

Let shoulders locked high, tight, recede.

Let feet cracked, worn, ease.

Let back, stiff, sore, bent open.

Let lungs swell breath like ocean.

Let all of us, all of us, all of us,   let all of us be unbroken.

Take heart. Earth hears every tremble touch. Feels each foot. Listens now.
Bring her justice, protection, peace.

By the sixth, extinction translates to which way the wind blows,   by
seventh, species are temporary, expendable,
                    nothing matches life.

                    Abalone, White Point Conception, to Punta Abreojos
marine snail, mollusk, spiral, sea ear, mother, bowl
                    Albatross, short tailed
 soaring on long, narrow wings, pink bill tipped bluish
                    Beetle, Casey's June
scarabs prefer alluvial fans, Sonoran desert scrub
                    Beetle, Mount Hermon June
Scarabaeidae in sandy soils Zayante Sand Hills
                    Butterfly, Behren's silverspot
upper golden under brown spotted silver/black
                    Butterfly, callippe silverspot
brushfoot hairy basal wing single annual flight
                    Butterfly, El Segundo blue
lays on coast buckwheat flowers, pollen nurtured
                    Butterfly, Lange's metalmark
from riverine sand dune, buckwheat bound
                    Butterfly, lotis blue
one-inch wingspans southwestern edge northern blue
                    Butterfly, mission blue
lay dorsal side lupine leaves
                    Butterfly, Myrtle's silverspot
lay on *viola* only, golf threatened
                    Butterfly, Palos Verdes blue
fog-shrouded, cool hills
                    Butterfly, Quino checkerspot
low-flying flutterer once most common
                    Butterfly, San Bruno elfin
swollen succulents entice
                    Butterfly, Smith's blue
dire, decimated from off-roading, livestock
                    Chub, bonytail

dark above, light below, desert fish
                    Chub, Owens tui
chunky, dorsal olive, bluish below
                    Condor, California
soar glide without wingbeat
                                        we attended first return in the eighties
here, carried, deep in mind's eye—free
                    Crayfish, Shasta
dual swimmerets over volcanic rubble
                    Fairy shrimp, conservancy
complex wave-like legs beat
                    Fairy shrimp, longhorn .
large stalked eyes, compound
                    Fairy shrimp, Riverside
vernal pool habitat, eggs tolerate heat, drought
                    Fairy shrimp, San Diego
seasonal rainfall dwellers
                    Flycatcher, southwestern willow
environmental degradation threatens
                            passerine, perching bird, yellow lower mandible
                    Fly, Delhi Sands flower-loving
Inland Empire, green-eyed
            first fly listed endangered
                                extinction brinked
                    Fox, San Joaquin kit
smallest North American dog
            petroleum threatened
                    Fox, San Miguel Island
Channel Islands, no wilds remain
                    Fox, Santa Catalina Island
            longest tail, largest size
                    Fox, Santa Cruz Island
dine on summer holly, rose, cholla,
            sumac, nightshade, deer mice, birds, crickets
                    Fox, Santa Rosa Island

golden eagles threaten, scarce
          Frog, mountain yellow-legged Northern
cryptic coloration, splotches like lichen
          Frog, mountain yellow-legged Southern
variable dorsal pattern, lacks vocal sacs
          Frog, Sierra Nevada yellow-legged
      shorter legged, eats dead
             generations go at once if water dries
          fewer frogs found, fewer grow legs, loose tails
          thrive

Goby, tidewater
Grasshopper, Zayante band-winged
Kangaroo rat, Fresno
Kangaroo rat, giant
Kangaroo rat, Morro Bay
Kangaroo rat, San Bernardino Merriam's
Kangaroo rat, Stephen's
Kangaroo rat, Tipton
Lizard, blunt-nosed leopard
Mountain beaver, Point Arena
Mouse, Pacific pocket
Mouse, salt marsh harvest
Pikeminnow, Colorado
Pupfish, desert
Pupfish, Owens
Rabbit, riparian brush
Rail, California clapper
Rail, light-footed clapper
Rail, Yuma clapper
Salamander, California tiger, Santa Barbara
Salamander, California tiger, Sonoma
Salamander, desert slender
Salamander, Santa Cruz long-toed
Salmon, coho
Sea turtle, leatherback
Sheep, Peninsular bighorn
Sheep, Sierra Nevada bighorn
Shrew, Buena Vista Lake ornate
Shrike, San Clemente loggerhead
Shrimp, California freshwater
Skipper, Carson wandering
Skipper, Laguna Mountains
Snail, Morro shoulderband
Snake, San Francisco garter
Steelhead, Southern California DPS
Stickleback, unarmored threespine
Sucker, Lost River
Sucker, razorback

Sucker, shortnose
quapdo, *recover, recover*
Tadpole shrimp, vernal pool
shielded carapace, predate fish
Tern, California least
millinery trade decimated
Tiger beetle, Ohlone
instars hatch green jewels
Toad, arroyo
sandy streamsides seal
Tui chub, Mohave
sole endemic Mojave River fish
Vireo, least Bell's
riparian, moth eater
Vole, Amargosa
salt cedar your nemesis, invasive

Whale, blue
Mysticeti, largest giant
heart big as bear
sacrificed for plastic
Whale, finback
giant second to blue
entanglement, vessel strike
unnatural sound impends
Whale, humpback
compose love songs, sing
serenade serenade serenade
slap water's surface drumming
breach dance, leap to fly
Whale, Sei
leave only fluke prints
Whale, sperm
paddle flippers
dive deep, nap,
stand to sleep

Wolf, gray
avoiding humans, return
of their own volition
                        Woodrat, riparian
                        dusky-footed woodrat
                        gray, cinnamon fur
                        tails furred, not scaly
Beetle, delta green ground
metallic, bronze, green jewels
grassland-playa pool matrix
                        Beetle, valley elderberry longhorn
                        Central Valley riparian forests
                        decimated, threatened
Butterfly, bay checkerspot
caterpillars eat purple owl's clover
                        Butterfly, Oregon silverspot
                        early blue-violet hosts
Cuckoo, yellow-billed Western
ku-ku-ku-ku-ku-kowip-kowip-
kowip-kowip neotropical migrant
                        Fairy shrimp, vernal pool
                        swim on backs, stroking eleven leg sets
Frog, California red-legged
largest Western native frog
                        Frog, Oregon spotted
                        upturned chartreuse eyes
Gnatcatcher, coastal California
flicks, hops tiny range, habitat now suburbs
                        Lizard, Coachella Valley fringe-toed
                        Blow sand ecosystem dependent
Lynx, Canada contiguous U.S. SPS
tufted ear tipped, bobtail
habitat stripped now suburbs
                        Moth, Kern primrose sphinx
                        stout diurnal moth eat baby blue-eyes
                        during drought go underground

Murrelet, marbled
exists in pairs, fish crustaceans
                Otter, southern sea
                oil spills recalculate lifespan
Owl, northern spotted
nocturnal, monogamous,
reside in older forests
                Plover, western snowy Pacific coastal pop
                buff, pale, pocket-sized shorebird on open beach
Salamander, California tiger
prefers in-ground burrows
                Salmon, Chinook California Coastal
                coastal stream deterioration
Salmon, So. Oregon coho—No. Cal Coast
dam construction, habitat degradation
                Seal, Guadalupe fur
                loss to hooking, entanglement, oil spills, development
Sea turtle, olive ridley
olive-green heart-shaped shell
fishing gear, climate change, egg thieves
                Smelt, delta
                San Francisco Bay Delta degradation
                smelt-down in the delta, ecosystem unravels
Snake, giant garter
sometimes infused with orange

Sparrow, San Clemente sage
dark streaks, dark cheeks
pigs, goats, military, cats
Steelhead, Central California Coast DPS
anadromous central coast riparian trout
climate change exacerbating issue
with dams, degradation
Steelhead, Northern California Coast DPS
winter / summer runs, stream temperature sensitivity
Sturgeon, green Southern DPS
can live to sixty, swimming marine
to fresh
Sucker, Santa Ana, three CA river basins
Seven Oaks Dam on the Santa Ana damaged habitat
Sucker, Warner
slender bodied, in shallow pools
Toad, Yosemite
warty skin, stocky, thick
can live twelve to fifteen years
Tortoise, desert, Mojave & Sonoran Deserts
columnar legs enjoy creosote bush flats
habitat destruction and poaching
leading to decline
Towhee, Inyo California
oldest known twelve years
ten months when banded
build nests in poison oak
dine on its pale white berries
feral burro foraging threatens
Trout, Lahontan cutthroat
stream spawner
endemic in Eastern California
Trout, Little Kern golden
olive to brass, flanks spotted
endemic in California, in isolation

早 early settlers transplanted
hybridization threatening existence
Trout, Paiute cutthroat
blush alongside your body
cattle graze, human recreation
subdue small stream network
Whipsnake, Alameda
human sprawl taking
taking, taking, taking
yellow racing striped
speeding shrub, chaparral
rodenticides, pesticides
herbicides, poison, poison

Little Kern golden trout,
                    rainbow overwhelms you.
All the caddis flies in Tulare
                    won't bring strength to tide.

Recently extinct:

California grizzly (*Ursus arctos californicus*) 1922

                    was shot in Tulare County, California

                    1924, grizzly maybe seen
                    Sequoia National Park

                    never again seen   in California.

                    Their native state.

                    State seals, flags bear Monarch

Bear Flag Revolt in Sonoma settlers wiped out the grizzly, uzamati

                    Red star, lone supergiant, Betelgeuse
                    supernova

                    what happens when stars die
                    death of a star death of a star

Sacramento Valley tiger beetle
Southern California kit fox

Clear Lake splittail
Tecopa pupfish
Thicktail chub

Mono Lake diving beetle
Pasadena freshwater shrimp
Sooty crayfish
Xerces blue butterfly

Remembering the lives before them,   we
broke into double-throated song scales
singing

                    nothing matches life,
                  recite   *their names now:*

                  Ramshaw Meadows abronia
San Mateo thorn-mint
                  San Diego thorn-mint
Cushenbury oxytheca
                  San Clemente Island bird's-foot trefoil
Santa Cruz Island bird's-foot trefoil
                  Santa Cruz Island lotus
Blasdale's bent grass / delisted
                  Munz's onion
Yosemite onion
                  Sonoma alopecurus
San Diego ambrosia
                  large-flowered fiddleneck
McDonald's rockcress
                  Baker's manzanita

The Cedars manzanita

Santa Rosa Island manzanita

Little Sur manzanita / delisted

Franciscan manzanita

Del Mar manzanita

Hearsts' manzanita

San Bruno Mountain manzanita

Presidio manzanita

Morro manzanita

Ione manzanita

Pacific manzanita

pallid manzanita

marsh sandwort

Humboldt milk-vetch

Cushenbury milk-vetch

Braunton's milk-vetch

Clara Hunt's milk-vetch

Lane Mountain milk-vetch

Long Valley milk-vetch

Coachella Valley milk-vetch

Fish Slough milk-vetch

Sodaville milk-vetch

Peirson's milk-vetch

Mono milk-vetch

Ventura Marsh milk-vetch

coastal dunes milk-vetch

Trask's milk-vetch

triple-ribbed milk-vetch

San Jacinto Valley crownscale

Bakersfield smallscale

Encinitas baccharis

bensoniella

Nevin's barberry

island barberry

Sonoma sunshine

Point Reyes blennosperma

dwarf goldenstar

Hoffman's rockcress

thread-leaved brodiaea
Kaweah brodiaea
Chinese Camp brodiaea
Indian Valley brodiaea
leafy reed grass
Dunn's mariposa lily
Siskiyou mariposa lily
Tiburon mariposa lily
Mariposa pussypaws
Stebbins' morning-glory
San Benito evening primrose
white sedge
Tompkins' sedge
tree-anemone
Tiburon paintbrush
succulent owl's-clover
ash-gray paintbrush
Mt. Gleason paintbrush
San Clemente Island paintbrush
soft-leaved paintbrush
Pitkin Marsh paintbrush
California jewel-flower
slender-pod jewel-flower / delisted
Coyote ceanothus
Hearsts' ceanothus
maritime ceanothus
Mason's ceanothus
Vail Lake ceanothus
Pine Hill ceanothus
Catalina Island mountain-mahogany
Santa Lucia purple amole
Camatta Canyon amole
salt marsh bird's-beak
soft bird's-beak
palmate-bracted bird's-beak
Howell's spineflower
Orcutt's spineflower
San Fernando Valley spineflower

Ben Lomond spineflower
        Monterey spineflower
                Scotts Valley spineflower
                        robust spineflower
                                        Sonoma spineflower
                Ashland thistle
        fountain thistle
    Chorro Creek bog thistle
Suisun thistle
        surf thistle
                La Graciosa thistle
                        Presidio clarkia
                                Vine Hill clarkia
                                        Merced clarkia
                        Pismo clarkia
                    Springville clarkia
            Mt. Diablo bird's-beak
        seaside bird's-beak
Pennell's bird's-beak
        Wiggins' croton
                bristlecone cryptantha
                    July gold
                        Red Rock tarplant
                                Livermore tarplant
                        Otay tarplant
                    Gaviota tarplant
            Santa Susana tarplant
        Mojave tarplant
Baker's larkspur
        Cuyamaca larkspur
                golden larkspur
                    San Clemente Island larkspur
                        Mount Laguna aster
                                Vandenberg monkeyflower
                    beach spectaclepod
            slender-horned spineflower
        Cuyamaca Lake downingia
Santa Clara Valley dudleya

short-leaved dudleya
      Agoura Hills dudleya
            Santa Monica dudleya
Santa Cruz Island dudleya
      Conejo dudleya
            Laguna Beach dudleya
            Santa Barbara Island dudleya
Verity's dudleya
      Ash Meadows daisy
      Kern mallow
            Big Bear Valley sandwort
        Santa Ana River woollystar
    Hoover's woolly-star / FDR (gray, no note)
Tracy's eriastrum
      Parish's daisy
         Indian Knob mountainbalm
          Lompoc yerba santa
      Trinity buckwheat
   Ione buckwheat
Irish Hill buckwheat
      Butterworth's buckwheat
      conejo buckwheat
         Santa Barbara Island buckwheat
      San Nicolas Island buckwheat
    Kellogg's buckwheat
southern mountain buckwheat
      Cushenbury buckwheat
      Thorne's buckwheat
         Twisselmann's buckwheat
      Congdon's woolly sunflower
    San Mateo woolly sunflower
San Diego button-celery
      Loch Lomond button-celery
      Delta button-celery
         Contra Costa wallflower
      Menzie's wallflower
    Santa Cruz wallflower
Hoover's spurge

Mexican flannelbush

Roderick's fritillary

Borrego bedstraw

El Dorado bedstraw

sand gilia

Boggs Lake hedge-hyssop

Orcutt's hazardia

Algodones Dunes sunflower

Butano Ridge cypress

Marin western flax

rock lady

water howellia

Webber's ivesia

Contra Costa goldfields

coast yellow leptosiphon

Congdon's lewisia

western lily

Parish's meadowfoam

Point Reyes meadowfoam

Pine Hill flannelbush

Gentner's fritillary

striped adobe-lily

box bedstraw

San Clemente Island bedstraw

Hoffmann's slender-flowered gilia

Ash Meadows gumplant

island rush-rose

Santa Cruz cypress

Gowen cypress

Lake County western flax

Santa Cruz tarplant

Tahquitz ivesia

Burke's goldfields

beach layia

San Francisco lessingia

Mason's lilaeopsis

Pitkin Marsh lily

Baker's meadowfoam

Butte County meadowfoam
Sebastopol meadowfoam
San Clemente Island woodland star
Mariposa lupine
The Lassics lupine
Milo Baker's lupine
Nipomo Mesa lupine
Father Crowley's lupine
Tidestrom's lupine
Truckee barberry / delisted
San Clemente Island bush-mallow
Santa Cruz Island bush-mallow
Santa Cruz Island malacothrix
island malacothrix
willowy monardella
San Joaquin woollythreads
Gambel's water cress
spreading navarretia
few-flowered navarretia
many-flowered navarretia
Twisselmann's nemacladus
Colusa grass
Amargosa nitrophila
Kneeland Prairie pennycress
Dehesa nolina
Eureka Dunes evening-primrose
Antioch Dunes evening-primrose
Bakersfield cactus
California Orcutt grass
San Joaquin Valley Orcutt grass
hairy Orcutt grass
slender Orcutt grass
Sacramento Orcutt grass
Baja California birdbush
Gander's ragwort

Layne's ragwort
Geysers panicum
Dudley's lousewort
white-rayed pentachaeta

      Lyon's pentachaeta
northern Channel Islands phacelia
      Brand's star phacelia / (gray, no note)
 Yreka phlox
      San Bernardino Mountains bladderpod
whitebark pine
      Yadon's rein orchid
San Francisco popcornflower
      Calistoga popcornflower
North Coast semaphore grass
      San Bernardino blue grass
Napa blue grass
        San Diego mesa mint
Santa Lucia mint
      Otay Mesa mint
Scotts Valley polygonum
      Black Rock potentilla (gray, no notes)
Hickman's cinquefoil
      Hartweg's golden sunburst
San Joaquin adobe sunburst
      Tahoe yellow cress
small-leaved rose
      adobe sanicle
rock sanicle
      Lake County stonecrop
Red Mountain stonecrop (gray, no notes)
      Santa Cruz Island winged-rockcress
Owens Valley checkerbloom
      Cuesta Pass checkerbloom
Parish's checkerbloom

Keck's checkerbloom

Kenwood Marsh checkerbloom

bird-foot checkerbloom

Scadden Flat checkerbloom

Red Mountain catchfly

Metcalf Canyon jewel-flower

Tiburon jewel-flower

California seablite

California dandelion

slender-petaled thelypodium

Santa Ynez false lupine

Santa Cruz Island fringepod

Hidden Lake bluecurls

showy rancheria clover

Pacific Grove clover

Monterey clover

Greene's tuctoria

Crampton's tuctoria or Solano grass

Red Hills vervain

big-leaved crownbeard

Look at This Blue

Mutant blue-eyed coyotes   chance mutation

      baby blues in nine coyotes suggesting proliferation
          silvery, brown-backed with icy blue eyes
     antenna ears turning, satellite-like, hearing voles

Santa Cruz, Sacramento, Point Reyes
     their apex predators mostly wolves,
           mountain lions, or killed by humans
Here, they are thriving, hunting
       blue   eyed   chance mutation

Amah Mutsun Land Trust
Restoring Indigenous knowledge and practices
to Popeloutchom ancestral homelands

restores role as environmental stewards
　　—surviving descendant families—
Indigenous people who survived the Santa Cruz and San Juan Bautista
missions

You think it's exhaustive now; this is partial recount.

Entire peoples missionized.

Father Serra founded, oversaw enslavement, torture,
rape, murder, worked to death—average lifespan
mission Indian   once taken, was seven
years, no matter arrival age. He celebrated the harvest of
souls of Indian children dying of European diseases in
his captivity.

Saint?

Seven-year lifespan, no matter age of missionization.
Worked to death and/or typhoid.

"Although the stated goal of the Missions was to return land to the
Indians, no land was ever provided. During the Mission period over
19,421 Indians died at Mission San Juan Bautista and approximately
150,000 Indians died in California."   —Amah Mutsun Tribal Band

"Indians found drunk or vagrant were arrested
on Sunday, imprisoned overnight in a corral,
and convicted on Monday. Because few could
afford to pay the fine, the jail was kept stocked full
of potential laborers. . . . Unable to pay the fines
for their convictions, the prisoners were
auctioned off in the 'slave market.'"   —Brendan C. Lindsay

"Los Angeles had its slave mart, as well as New
Orleans and Constantinople—only the slave at
Los Angeles was sold fifty-two times a year as
long as he lived."   —Horace Bell

"the City Marshal and his assistants
. . . spend the Sabbath in arresting and
imprisoning Indians, supposed to be drunk. . . .
Now, we have no heart to do the Marshal the
slightest prejudice, but this leading off Indians and
locking them up over night, for the purpose of
taking away one of their paltry dollars, seems to us a
questionable act."   —Los Angeles Star

Sutter's Gold Rush set stage for state
                              slaughter
Sacramento River bloodied red wash
                              typical, from lifeline ripped
from innocents, 600-800 Indians enslaved by him

keeping in line with conquistadors
                    Native murders, massacres, enslavement
began long before others were also perpetrated upon.

Native slavery in Florida, 1596, a drop in the well of manifest
                    rivering the continent—the whole of it—
forget the manmade Panama Canal. Consider the absolute length
                    enslavement, massacre, murder.

California, free-soil state upon statehood,
                    sold Indians as common practice still.

Indian Act of 1850, California legislature authorized arrests
                    of any *vagrant* Natives to be *hired out* to highest bidder.
Native children to be indentured, before a justice of the peace,
                    by any white persons who wished for laborers.

"The value of the captives depends upon age, sex, beauty, and usefulness," wrote Calhoun. "Good looking females, not having passed the 'sear and yellow leaf,' are valued from $50 to $150 each; males, as they may be useful, one-half less, never more."

"That a war of extermination will continue to be waged between the races until the Indian race becomes extinct must be expected," he told legislators in the second state of the state address in 1851. "While we cannot anticipate this result but with painful regret, the inevitable destiny of the race is beyond the power or wisdom of man to avert."
    —Peter Hardeman Burnett, the state's first governor

Tenderloin mornings.
Someone took a shot at me before 9 a.m.
It's been two days since neighbors
shot over me, lying over you,
protecting you,
since Travelers Aid allowed me to
get here to take cover.
At least your father can't kill me now.
This passing car, mad at the world,
taking potshots, has poor aim,
or didn't mean to score.
Just trying to get some juice,
keep hydrated, my sister
still awake from her night shift
watching you for the first time
for ten minutes while I cross
Hyde, then Turk, grab a box of juice,
piece of bread, head back, unscathed.
Pass by the old man someone brought
from a reservation, left here
on the street. No one knows his
language. My sister says he'll accept
a sandwich, juice, so I go back, grab him one,
too. Today it's orange. *Here's a heel.* Someone
from St. Vincent's gave him a cane. He looks
maybe blind, or cataracted. Wish his name
was known. Wish we knew his home, get
him with his people. Morning seems
high above. The buildings block out
any rise and the whole thing seems
to spin cardinal points opposite
so north is south. Peninsula
living—Yelamu—Ramaytush,
Ohlone, my sister learns at SFSU,
works late shift, printing newspapers,

working for a bachelors in Native Studies,
takes her about eleven years complete.

Me, I'm scrambling just to hydrate, acclimate.
In the year Tom Petty wails, I *said*,
you don't have to live like a refugee.
Score before Care Not Cash SF labeled me indigent,
didn't offer a home, just rent to my sister.
In a few weeks you'll have red measles,
not move for days, dehydrated, will nearly
leave. From me standing in line, St. Vincent's,
with you wrapped tightly in sling alongside,
for food, medicine, essentials we don't keep.
The stream of morning over your face,
when you recover.

We're 7th/8th gen
shirttails undeserving,

unenrolled unfit undocumented
two gens from fluencies,

                    heritage,
but the Friendship House reps say we're welcome
to sit in   if we get over Oakland way.

This is before I could express
myself. Chin still positioned,
ready. Or chin down, ghosting
into horizons you can't see here.

My sister came here in the
seventies. Our mom and dad
for their honeymoon after
blind-date meeting in San Diego
in late forties. Last century.
You can feel them here, still.
Each time it's real, we call,
note space, *yes, we were there.*

Before any time passes, we
realize other families don't
have these homing knowns.

My sister is embarrassed of me.
Too backwoods. Too field laborer.
Too sharecropping. Too fisher.
Too farmer. Too backwoods.
Mocks my handiwork. Asks if
I plan to sell trinkets on the
side of the road. Maybe leather-
work, I claim. Show her mine.

She walks a block ahead of me
mocking me to her city friends.
Like we walked aisles over
from our mom, deep in delusion,
cursing through aisles in *Piggly Wiggly,*
but never mocking her. Not once.
Where did this mocking come from?
Raven cry (for my heart).

Here, streets lined with fresh
refugees, straggler homeless, cardboard
box men, prostitutes, pimps, beautiful
neighborhood people who teach me
you can get a great meal for $2 on
this block. How to eat with chopsticks,
which store gives free bread if you
don't have $. Lots of Skins pass through.
Not Ohlone.

Indian Country, California, every bit.

      Under U.S. law,
      over a hundred rancherias, reserved spaces, trust allotments
               more than ribbon state fabric, more original weave

No other state has more original peoples residing
               one-hundred-nine nations, federal recognition
seventy-eight petitioners

Genocide did not begin at the rush for gold.
               Spanish missionaries, settlers, ranchers

Still, estimates of fatalities exist:
               300,000 to 250,000 Spanish-rule killed
               250,000 to 150,000 under Mexico
               Under US, after 1848

               in two years of gold fever, 100,000 killed.
of 150,000 people, 20,000 more killed in the next 25 years,
               when *the state spent $1.7 million to murder*
16,000.
      When the state—

When its mission missionized

How many villages could be missionized, enslaved for one mission?
Led by Father Junípero Serra
Father Estévan Tapís

Santa Inez Mission:
Achillimo, Aguama, Ahuamhoue, Akachumas, Akaitsuk,
Alahulapgas, Alizway, Asiuhuil, Awashlaurk, Calahuasa, Cascel,
Cholicus, Chumuchu, Coloc, Geguep, Guaislac, Huhunata,
Hunawurp, Ialamne, Ionata, Jonatas, Kalak, Kalawashuk,
Katahuac, Kulahuasa, Kuyam, Matiliha, Mekewe, Mishtapawa,
Nipoma, Nutonto, Sapelek, Saptuui, Sauchu, Shopeshno,
Sikitipuc, Sisuchi, Situchi, Sotonoemu, Souscoc, Stucu, Suiesia,
Suktanakamu, Tahijuas, Takuyumam, Talaxano, Tapanissilac,
Tarkepsi, Tekep, Temesathi, Tequepis, Tinachi, Tsamala,
Tujanisuissilac.

San Miguel Island:
Nimollollo, Zaco.

Santa Rosa Island:
Kshiwukciwu, Lilibeque, Muoc, Ninumu, Níquesesquelua,
Niquipos, Patiquilid, Patiquiu, Pilidquay, Pisqueno, Poele,
Siliwihi.

Santa Cruz Island:
Alali, Chalosas, Chosho, Coycoy, Estocoloco, Hahas,
Hitschowon, Klakaamu, Lacayamu, Liyam, Macamo, Mashcal,
Mishumac, Nanahuani, Niakla, Nichochi, Nilalhuyu, Nimatlala,
Nimitapal, Nitel, Nomkolkol, Sasuagel, Xugua.

San Buenaventura Mission:

Aguin, Alloc, Anacbuc, Chihucchihui, Chumpache, Eshulup, Kachyayakuch, Kanwaiakaku, Kinapuke, Lacayamu, Liam, Lisichi, Lojos, Luupsch, Mahow, Malahue, Malico, Matilhja, Miguihui, Miscanaka, Piiru, Sespe, Shishalap, Simi. Sisa, Sisjulcioy, Sissabanonase, Soma, Tapo, Ypuc, Yxaulo.

Purísima Mission:

Alacupusyuen, Ausion, Esmischue, Esnispele, Espiiluima, Estait, Fax, Guaslaique, Huasna, Huenejel, Huenepel, Husistaic, Ialatnma, Jlaacs, Kachisupal, Lajuchu, Lipook, Lisahuats, Lompoc, Nahuey, Naila, Ninyuelgual, Nocto, Omaxtux Pacsiol, Paxpili, Sacsiol, Sacspili, Salachi, Sihimi, Silimastus, Silimi, Silino, Silisne, Sipuca, Sisolop, Sitolo, Stipu, Suntaho, Tutachro.

Santa Barbara Mission:

Alcax, Alican, Alpincha, Alwathalama, Amolomol, Anejue, Awhawhilashmu, Cajats, Cajpilili, Casalic, Cashwah, Chiuchin, Cholosoc, Chuah, Cinihuay, Cuyamus, Eleunaxciay, Eljman, Eluaxcu, Estuc, Geliac, Gleuaxcuqu, Guainonost, Guina, Hanava, Hello, Huelemin, Huililoc, Huixapapa, Humalija, Hunxapa, Inajalaihu, Inojey, Ipec, Ituc, Lagcay, Laycayamu, Lintja, Lisuchu, Lugups, Majalayghua, Mishtapalwa, Mistaughchewaugh, Numguelgar, Otenashmoo, Salpilel, Sayokinck, Sihuicom, Silpoponemew, Sinicon, Sisahiahut, Sisuch, Snihuax, Sopone, Taxlipu, Texmaw, Xalanaj, Xalou.

Miscellaneous:

Anacoat, Anacot, Antap, Aogni, Asimu, Bis, Caacat, Casnahacmo, Casunalmo, Cayeguas, Chwaiyok, Cicacut, Ciucut, Ciyuktun, Elquis, Escumawash, Garomisopona, Gun, Helapoonuch, Honmoyaushu, Hueneme, Humkak, Immahal, Isha, Ishgua, Kamulas, Kasaktikat, Kashiwe, Kashtok, Kashtu, Kaso, Katstayot, Kaughii, Kesmali, Koiyo, Kuiyamu, Lohastahni, Mahahal, Malhokshe, Malito, Malulowoni, Maquinanoa, Masewuk, Mershom, Michiyu, Micoma, Misesopano, Mishapsna, Misinagua, Mismatuk, Mispu, Mugu, Mupu, Nacbue, Nipomo, Nocos, Ojai, Olesino, Onkot, Onomio, Opia, Opistopia, Paltatre, Partocac, Potoltuc, Pualnacatup, Quanmugua, Quelqueme, Quiman, Salnahakaisiku, Sapaquonil, Saticoy, Satwiwa, Shalawa, Shalkahaan, Shisblaman, Sholikuwewich, Shuku, Shup, Shushuchi, Shuwalashu, Simomo, Sisichii, Sitaptapa, Siuktun, Skonon, Spookow, Sulapiu, Susuquey, Sweteti, Swino, Tallapoolina, Temeteti, Tocane, Topotopow, Tukachkach, Tushumu, Upop, Walektre, Wihatset, Xabaagua, Xagua, Xocotoc, Yutum.

Chumash Tribe

The Santa Rosa islanders, of the Chumashan family of California.

How many massacres?

Sacramento River Massacre
Klamath Lake Massacre
Sutter Buttes Massacre
Pauma Massacre
Temecula Massacre
Rancheria Tulea Massacre
Kern and Sutter Massacres
Konkow Maidu Slaver Massacre
Bloody Island Massacre
Mariposa War Massacre
Old Shasta Town Massacre
Bridge Gulch Massacre
Wright Massacre
Howonquet Massacre
Yontocket Massacre
Achulet Massacre
Ox Incident Massacre
Klamath River Massacres
Shingletown Massacre
Round Valley Settler Massacre
Jarboe's War Massacre
Pit River Massacre
Chico Creek Massacre
Massacre at Bloody Rock
Indian Island Massacre
Keyesville Massacre
Konkow Trail of Tears Massacre
Oak Run Massacre
Owens Lake Massacre
Three Knolls Massacre
Camp Seco Massacre
Kingsley Cave Massacre

Land of the—

war crimes, crimes against humanity, genocide

without limitations, statute.

Solution set out in Vizenor's
        tribunals
                assembled in the academy, investigated, fully researched
trials, for the premeditated serial genocide committed through government
role/s.

Call for country, accountability, justice.

California, California

A few cattle lost, probably killed by white men, began the basis of massacre.
State-sponsored—

1856–1859 Round Valley Settler Massacres:
White settlers killed 1000+ Yuki over three years in separate massacres.

1859–1860 Jarboe's War:
Eel River Rangers / white settlers led by Walter Jarboe killed
at least 283 Indian men
countless Indian women and children.

U.S. Government reimburses their costs.

1860 Indian Island:
80–250 Wiyot killed by white settlers in three near simultaneous assaults
Humboldt County, California. Mostly women, children, elders were
massacred.

1863 Konkow Trail of Tears:
August, 1863, Konkow Maidu ordered sent to Bidwell Ranch in Chico,
then to Round Valley Reservation at Covelo. Any remaining to be shot.
Rounded up and marched, west of Sacramento Valley 461 began the walk
277 finished on the 18th of September, 1863.

1864 Oak Run Massacre: California settlers massacred 300 Yana
gathered for spiritual ceremony near the head of Oak Run.

45 tribal communities of formerly recognized
California tribes terminated in United States
Termination policy in the 1950s.
Tribal communities never recognized by US.

In 1994, the state of California recognized the Tongva
"as the aboriginal tribe of the Los Angeles Basin."
Senate Bill 1134

2017, Governor Jerry Brown first California
governor to acknowledge a state-sponsored
genocide.

It's called a genocide. That's what it was. A genocide.
[There's] no other way to describe it and that's the way it
needs to be described in the history books. And so I'm here
to say the following: I'm sorry on behalf of the state of
California. 2019, Governor Gavin Newsom

Newsom also established a "truth and healing council"
to provide Native perspectives on the historical record. The
council will include tribal representatives and others and
issue a report on the historical relationships between
Native Californians and the state of California.

In 2020-2021, during the pandemic, COVID-19, former Yolo
deputy sheriff, bigot, sponsors petition to recall Newsom.

The state's first legislative session gave white settlers the
ability to take custody of Native children, arrest Native
peoples at will and enslave them for petty "crimes."

For Indians and Indian Country there are special
rules that govern state and local jurisdiction.
There may also be federal and tribal laws that apply.

Chinese Massacre
           Golden Dragon Massacre

Thousand Oaks Shooting   *San Ysidro McDonald's Massacre*
                San Bernardino Attack
Pacific Air Lines Flight 773 Mass Murder–Suicide
California Genocide, 9492 to 16,094 killed in massacres

        1846–1873 over 120,000 died overall during state sponsored period
California leads
mass pop-pop-pop

COVID-19 times
firings fell first year

come
worst to first
pandemic ratios

What's the gun-incident-ratio for falling illness?
        First time someone placed
        pistol grip in my hand
        was roulette challenge

                You?

How many times was I given up, left
for dead   rejected   objectified   ejected
does it matter, still   when

jump-started   or just woke when unexpected to
always returning to the beauty of this world
abject misery layered   still splendor despite
beautiful/horrendous   juxtapositioning
throughout time

Look at This Blue

Mission blue butterfly   *from coastal chaparral, grasslands,*
                    Mission District San Francisco, Twin Peaks, Marin
                    County
                    most upon San Bruno Mountain
              small, delicate gossamer-winged
              male, iridescent blue-lavender
              female, dark brown, blue base
              fringed in long, white hair-like scales
              undersides spotted
              wingspread 1-1.5 inches
caterpillars solely ingest native California lupine,
eat silver, summer, varicolor   lupine,
    adults drink flower nectar, buckwheat, golden asters, wild hyacinths
endangered first by development;
    public infrastructure development projects remain significant threat

The civil rights of nonwhites were so contentious that California failed to ratify the 14th and 15th Amendments—granting citizenship to former slaves and ensuring the rights of black men to vote—until the middle of the 20th century

California banned slavery in 1849. California law allowed
Native people to be enslaved in 1910.

*1999, Ishi's brain returned to his closest living relatives,
the Yana people*

*Twenty-four immigrants have died in ICE custody, by August 2019,
during 45.*

At least seven children since late 2018.

*Since January 2019, more than ninety people have died
encountering US BORDER AGENTS.* Three California related.

Over 130 fatal encounters with CBP since 2010

Use of the largest federal law enforcement entity
U.S. Customs and Border Protection (CBP)

Use of force
Use of ignorance
Use of weapons
Use of fascism
Use of projectiles
Use of asphyxiation
Use of taser
Use of fists
Use of feet
Use of chemical agent
Use of high-speed chase

Use of inadequate medical attention
Use of medical emergencies
Use of homicide
Use of fear
Use of aggression
Use of terror
Use of depression
Use of drowning
Use of heat
Use of cold
Use of privilege
Use of history
Use of future
Use of economics
Use of education
Use of power
Use of language
Use of literacy
Use of literature
Use of poverty
Use of situation
Use of attitude
Use of annoyance
Use of knee-jerk reaction
Use of anger
Use of weather
Use of water
Use of nutrition
Use of supplies
Use of pharmaceuticals
Use of essential needs
Use of shelter
Use of foreigner
Use of alien
Use of mistaken identity

Use of homecoming
Use of family visitation
Use of parental duty
Use of condition
Use of discretion
Use of fabrication
Use of collision
Use of withholding
Use of position
Use of brutality
Use of border crossing

Use of lack of conviction of any on-duty agent
   in the ninety-year history of the agency

She left her children
with her mother
He didn't have ID
They were in a car
Suspicious
Severe dehydration
She needed insulin
He had pneumonia
He had pneumonia
He had pneumonia
He needed heart medicine
He had a seizure
   after agents secured him
reportedly
Children in border detention
   have contracted Coronavirus
reportedly
20,427 total confirmed COVID-19 cases
   in border custody, facility
1,025 in current isolation

reportedly
They were turned away while
    attempting to donate diapers, hygienic supplies,
        sanitizers, toys, toothbrushes, books, clothing,
            masks, gloves, bottled water
The agent spiked water jugs
    left for asylum seekers crossing desertways
The second agent flipped them
    emptying the contents
He was in the middle of a divorce
    when he shot the migrant teen
They were Salvadoran
    She was Honduran
He was Guatemalan

They were Indian American
She was Cuban
  He was American
She was Mexican
  He was Congolese
They were Nicaraguan
  She was Colombian
Nationality unknown   unknown   unknown
She was Canadian
  He was a U.S. citizen
She was an American citizen
  He was a long-term California resident
In the case of brutality
  Officer logged in fear of life
No weapon was found
  Two were alleged suicides
Failure to provide adequate care
  Shot in the back twice, then killed
    by the border agent
The teen was noted as seriously ill
  when they locked him in, secured the cell

Shot and killed standing on the bank throwing rocks
  Foot chased into the lake, they drowned there
Shot multiple times in the back for throwing rocks
  for insubordination
He was taken to a holding cell following arrest
  in six hours he was dead

"I want David Villalobos' name out there," said his younger sister, Brittany Villalobos. "I want it out there and I want there to be noise."

their names

All along the wall Indigenous remains were unearthed from centuries of rest
we are restless

Not breaking this up for comfort.

She remembered stories, grandmas watching over
    from long ago. Still here, singing comfort –

Evening, on the chaparral

rain-soaked creosote releases   smoky scent
    lingers under Pleiades, coming up on buck moon.

Our governess, she reduces inflammation,
rids fungus,   her twigs, bark, teas
    hold mysteries,   toxins, medicinal

    properties, unfenced, unwalled, growing
for anyone to reap,   moon lights her tips like

Pleiades, seven little goats, little eyes, seven sisters,
    Subaru, pearls, hen with chicks, united.
      Taken there, held, or forever running from maddened machismo,
        forever unchecked – forever.

Rainy stars, sailing stars, mapping out navigation
accompanied by dual forces, often parental,
    one turns invisible at will.

She was invisible for a while.
    Headlined for an hour
between the lists of COVID-19 deaths, hospitalizations,
    cases soaring in encampments, detentions,
between borders, nations, between worlds – hope.

Kids running from agents, she lost her way, step,
    before being thrown into the freezer
assigned foil for blanket, shivering through shimmering night.

Mama

Lodged in the spine.
Lodged in the neck.
Lodged in the abdomen.
Lodged in the skull.

Unlodged, slept on concreted curb.
Unlodged, covered themselves with creosote branches.
Unlodged, pulled shirt over head to sleep.
Unlodged, they expired.

State of the State.
Homelessness increased remarkably

If we were only Otay Mountain lotus
   butterflies, maybe

why did you come
we love California
our spouses are here
our children
grandmothers
work
our lives

His country of origin
     Vietnam
admitted as lawful, permanent resident
     1984
final order of removal
     2004
     2005
released on supervision
     2017
found guilty of disorderly conduct
  upon imprisonment, denied medical issue
was taking prescription for schizophrenia
  for major depressive disorder
     2018
transferred, unresponsive, no reflexes, gag or pupils

The preliminary cause of death was myocardial infarction
  multiple blocked arteries

The Armenian married to a U.S. citizen, was pronounced dead.
The preliminary cause of death is
hypertensive and atherosclerotic
cardiovascular disease, and the manner of
death was natural

The video findings of the final days of a sixteen-year-old
  do not match the agents' account

How much does a short story earn a writer?

California on Friday sued the Trump administration to
challenge the legality of a new "public charge" rule that could
deny green cards to immigrants who receive public assistance,
including food stamps, Medicaid and housing vouchers.
August 2019, LA Times

California and 19 other states sue over rule under 45 allowing prolonged detention for asylum seekers—August 2019

Held anyway without consent, mutually fit, nothing but wrong.

My gut aches. All this, all this indelible hurt.

A scrub jay calls for peanuts, whole, raw, shell intact.
Each year a pair leaves one, takes one with. Our bird stays,
plays with squirrels, takes nuts from us, coexists.

Trusts.

Where is the love for young ones taken, without reason, hope?

Machine state racking up torture tendencies, kids dying inside
the State, not inside the state. California over rule, overrule.
Find freedom for all. Housing for all. Education for all. Make this
a free state despite the State.

For 50th time, California sues the Trump administration—
"That's a lot of lawsuits"   —California Attorney General Xavier Becerra

The lawsuits range from fighting the diversion of emergency
dollars to fund a border wall and environmental protection
rollbacks, as well as contesting the dismantling of the
Affordable Care Act and banning transgender people from the
military.   —May 2019, Sacramento Bee

Trump sued California on Tuesday over a new law requiring presidential
candidates to release their tax returns to run in the state's primary
elections.   —August 2019, Reuters

"A 2,000-mile wall is a monument to stupidity, not just vanity,
to stupidity," Newsom said. "It's pure political theater. He
creates these sideshows, this political theatre, this political
grandstanding."   —California Governor Gavin Newsom,
                                             March 2019, CBS Los Angeles

California has joined with 21 other states, the District of
Columbia, Los Angeles, and five other cities in a legal
challenge to the Trump administration's repeal of Obama-era
clean power rules.

"This is not just about fighting Donald Trump," said Newsom.
"This is about our kids and our grandkids. This is about clean
air, clean water and endangered species."   —KQED

Glacial melt, waves and waves.

                                    100 times faster than previously imagined.

Ice, half the planet away, sheets

                                 lost on edges of continents

                                 rise levels, half a meter more

massive accelerating increase

                                 1.5 millimeters per year plus this new ice melt

We're all sitting on ground near enough what might go under, liquify,
on what used to be an ocean, could be

                                 shells still testify—

Four bodies found floating from dive-boat fire
Twenty more below the deck
dozens missing, lost.

                                 Channel Islands Labor Day cruise—
                                 Conception burned while mooring.

Crew, awake, jumped to safety.
My son was on that boat, someone said.

Conducting shoreline searches for any new survivors.
No one is calling out; it is still, quiet.
                              The *Grape Escape* helping rescue.

Asked if crew tried to help passengers,   *I don't have answers.*
The call was garbled, it was not clear.
                              Mayday. The boat fully ablaze.

Bow still visible

                              vessel sank in sixty-four feet of water.
3:15 a.m., the call came.

Antarctica counts for 10% of all ocean level rise.

                                        Greenland 20%.

somewhere   highly crevassed ice is falling.

On ice summit, rain met ice

                         first fall recorded. First touch.

Glaciers sitting below sea level, breaking off, breaking.

                                hard to find open air

in the midst of so many glacial breaks, floating by.

Glaciers flowing directly into oceans.

                            Their component, contribution

to rising levels.

                    El Niño can worsen flooding, disrupt wetlands.

Rise

the prophesied child, boy, one of 270,000 shelterless California K-12 kids
                                        last year, the first of COVID-19,
his hand shot through, shot, playing where he lives, camp,
                            Oakland, land of acorn mush, hush

don't remember the times tumbles whirred to stop
                         to sleep warm, when washers left
climb in, pull door to, hope nobody closes tight
                      night

absence barred souls
                  locked up   slept despair measled
slung like bundles
                  like this boy   his chin positioned to scoop
day away like any other, this year, this draw, this whittled life

restrained on his stomach five minutes
pinned by Alameda police
gone   gone

You were so sick, so internally embattled
                              suddenly a soft touch to the shoulder
ghost, maybe, until you glimpsed the opossum's so-soft front foot
                         offering solace, companionship
                                   touch in the time of despair

mercy   mercy *woah-ah mercy mercy*
            me

           Perforating heart, lung, liver
Los Angeles County Coroner—shot twice—
         woah mercy mercy

Storm swell, high tide, soak

                    surge significant seawater over coast,
pushed waters over coastal riprap

the ocean's going to win.
Caught by a strong wave

                    once went out so far, so deep, couldn't see

surface from bottom, shore was mystery.   Spectacular waves loose—
1989 Loma Prieta earthquake

                    will be less costly than 2025 rise.

It's all leaving.   Divers sleep in a single room of bunk beds   none of
them in sight.

Shots fired at panga boat, smuggling
                                    marijuana into a legal state, illegally
                                    bales overboard,   still searching.

A bill requires training for officers in
                                    de-escalating confrontations

power line to a tower fail

                        in known wind conditions.

Lawsuits for Pacific Gas & Electric, in wildfires

faulty equipment, negligence made.
                                    Surveillance

Poway synagogue, Gilroy Garlic Festival,
                                    semiautomatic, he cut through fence to
kill

horrific, gun-violence epidemic
San Fernando man shot his family
                                    parents, brother, friend   a bus
Poway, a rabbi shot in both hands, AR-15
                                    woman protecting him killed
shrapnel, *a bit of twisted irony.*

Look at This Blue

Blue Whale   *alongside Monterrey, San Diego, Baja*
                    gentle giant heaviest animal to ever live on earth, twice
                    Argentinosaurus
          ship strikes kill eleven per year, U.S. West Coast, with ship increase
population will be depleted, noise, military testing, sonic battery,
          chemicals, plastics
                    krill, anchovy, tiny fish, tiny crustaceans absorb
                    microplastics
                              a blue whale eats between two and four tons
                              of krill per day

                              —blue with belly full of plastics—

Indian children traded, sold

bid, early 1900 a law still refused
                            difference between apprenticeship
                            slavery
Indian children unprotected under any laws
                            special laws written to master

Children's home means any institution, dwelling, house, tent.

(1890), the California Supreme Court ruled that public school
        districts in California may not establish separate schools
                    for children of African descent.

(1890) Mr. Horatio N. Rust was instructed by the Commissioner of Indian
Affairs
                            to find a suitable site in Southern California
                            for an Indian school, separate from other
                            children
                            and their own families
                            Perris Indian School opened 1892
                            became Sherman Institute 1903

1971 became accredited and known as Sherman Indian High School

Those who died there were often buried in the school cemetery.

*May 3 marks an old tradition amongst the local
tribes where many local reservations decorate
their cemeteries with flowers and replace old
crosses. Sherman Indian High School designates
this as Indian Flower Day*

he fell under freight train during escape
typhoid ended them
broken heart
broken

*In 1852, California legislators passed a harsh fugitive slave
law that condemned dozens of African American migrants to
deportation and lifelong slavery.*

THE CHINESE EXCLUSION ACT OF 1882 was signed into law on
May 6, 1882.

"An act to execute certain treaty stipulations relating to Chinese"

prohibited the immigration of Chinese laborers for ten years.

Deprived, defrauded,
                    their property embezzled for trains, cars, buses,
                    planes, expended
to deport people from the neighborhood, with no due cause,
                    no right to due process, no justice under the law.

Beginning in 1929, the State of California forcibly removed
                              400,000 Mexican American people
                              from their state,
         their country of birth.   Enacting threats, committing
                              violent acts, raiding targeted persons,
                        misnaming them illegal aliens,
                    despite legal residence, citizenship.

This chapter may be cited as the
    "Apology Act for the 1930s Mexican Repatriation Program." 8721.

The Legislature finds and declares

for the fundamental violations
    of their basic civil liberties and constitutional rights committed
during the period of illegal deportation and coerced emigration.

    The State of California apologizes

The State of California
    regrets
        the suffering and hardship endured as a direct result of
    the government sponsored Repatriation

The State defamed, robbed, banished neighbors
so many places counted the hours, days, years,   most often there, became
            silhouette lines in Griffith Park, Tule Lake, Manzanar,
                        bags tagged Woodland, Turlock, Tulare, Stockton,
rations read San Bruno, Salinas, Sacramento,
            babies born Pomona, Pinedale, Owens Valley,
elders passed Merced, Fresno, Arcadia, or loaded on trains, departed –
            Like horses, left in Santa Anita Racetrack stables, Tanforan
racetrack
                        –Tanforan–8033 detained, interned.
Tanforan nights spent on haysack beds, stinky stalls, rank from manure.
            Miné fresh from exhibiting and curating in San Francisco MoMA
Here, her UC Berkeley MA, art/anthropology
            documented detainees in charcoal, watercolor, tempura.
1912, born/raised Riverside, California. Banned from living on the west
coast, 1942.
            Executive Order 9066: Resulting in the Relocation of Japanese
Citizen 13660
Miné Okubo, Nisei

The fat cats she offered, a glimpse of humanity to calm despair.

            Citizen 13660 (1946)—American Book Award (1984)

The Civil Liberties Act of 1988, *Restitution for World War II internment
of Japanese-Americans and Aleuts*

apologize on behalf of the people
                                discourage injustices
                                                make restitution

to citizens, resident aliens, Aleuts of Pribilof Islands
for all taken, taken, taken, taken, occupied, or destroyed

discourage future violations of civil liberties
Make credible, make sincere, concern

In the field, forced to crawl through culvert, water neck-high, floating
      no way to maneuver, with a child through this

to escape immersion, criminals, violence, to find peace
      find home, find dreaming.

Like clouds pulling into towers, we gathered,
      all of us. They made us throw out the suitcase
we brought, made us leave the known

      empty ourselves, for something promised
now a threat. I remember spare-changing with him on second floor
      watching that I bring enough in.

Your earnest face. Asking me, "Where is he?"
      "How about you and I leave, I buy you a dinner, you get away?"
My emptiness void of belief such was real,

      "Even a quarter?" hand extended.
                            I still think of you sometimes.

When he busted my face, oftentimes, my diligence went unnoticed.
When he claimed I was in car wrecks
                    his mom believed.
                    Nearly killed me in one, so must be
                    must be a car wreck every other week, each time
                    purple faded, teeth repaired, gauze removed
                    bruised from brow to jaw, pummeled
                    what a mess

Those who rage are full of emptiness, hollow people, unfilled, vacant.
                Hate fulfills the space, festers there, blooms.
                    Vacancy blinked neon in motor court windows
like his eyes, heart,   was it a heart? No heart.

Something in me could care less now. Something in my rearranged
appearance
fits my unfittedness,   signals *this one can be*   don't be fooled,
I have a way out.

In the bus on the way to retraining for field workers.

We left Santa Paula for Ventura daily.

Rhododendron, eucalyptus, Limoneira orange groves, peppers,
flowers for Burpee Seed Company
red-winged hawks every mile
of eucalyptus 126 Ventura Highway
on watch, like us, for movement.

x

Santa Paula. North star of Guanajuato.
Mupu of Chumash.
We escaped here. Refugees. Closed eyes,
let finger configure map, conjure home.   This is where.
From here everything changes.   Rewrite, reset, reverb.
Offer projects for Santa Ynez kids at get-go.   Offer self.
Send for my folks to follow.   Dad notes, know this—
if there is snow on Topatopa, everything's okeh.

Mom doesn't leave the pickup until the fourth day.
Vallejo apartment, their last place West   Coast. Way prior
to my lifetime.

Restful now, restart. Gratitude.
So lucky to have had a dad.

Vista del Mar
resort asylum we deliver
                                    her
                                                to begin anew   life   I
picked lock when she bolted
                                    drove her north to find peace midst
schizophrenia with California persuasion
                                    first time in facility without a state embrace.
first time without electroshock, without abuse, without malice there
                                    where we left her
so many times
                                    Here she begins
                                    new

Your father released from prison
for voice-modulated arson tell-all.
He would knock over someone, something,
                              force me into a car to drive him
we would be chased, careen, pulled over,
                              he would jump out with sawed-offs ready
walk straight up to them
                    tell them what they would tell their dispatch
                    and they would.

            I never knew him before he assaulted me.

Your arm was twisted, bone exposed
face past point of wet   stained,
                              fledgling fell there

"He wouldn't stop crying, so he's been sitting here since lunch."

That was the final day you were left-prominent
                    all bland shaming, "Big boys don't use their left hand"
"The class scissors are made for right-hands"
          suddenly would satisfy same teacher who marched you
here and complained about the noise
          after the class favorite broke your arm on monkey bars.

Like me, when the boy sucker round-housed me coming around hall corner.
          Upper force, lifted me off, hard land on knee moved the cap
                    blood everywhere from fully laid out nose
first teacher on the scene, invokes surname, "clean up this mess."

Schools were made to break us.

Santa Paula Bank on Harvard, was it?

                    Dad, deaf, spoke out loud, *Where did everyone go?*
while tellers duck, cover.

                        While robber
displays his weapon to me, gestures at my toddler,

suggest I gather.

                      I motion toward Dad
gesturing his deafness, offer to gather him as well,

                              mercy, with peace,

from the bank robber who escapes on a bicycle
                      about the time tellers
              remember him from high school.

On Jurupa a bike laid flat, crashed out
                              up against curb
just below his awkwardly posed   corpse
                    was the sense of it
something crude, a twisting, limb thrusting rigid, blue—
                    spread out in some complex tangle, unnatural
under sign for childcare center thirty feet from his fall.
                    He must have flipped there, over handlebars
like a child might, striking concrete too fast, too hard,
                    this man maybe heart attack, maybe assaulted.
his clothes worn, raggedy, last testament, homeless, maybe.
                    We moved to prayer in moment, called 9-1-1,
begged for mercy

begged for peace, sympathy for miserable
the river-bottom people   begged

                    for when we were them

scruffed, scuffed, sleeping under overpass, in dryers
to keep warm, kids, we were

                    under shattered skies,
dogs licking our faces, all we knew of love, here.
Each Chihuahua, every four-legged,

                  under arms, held close

every homeless leaning into shade in swelter
we worry about water

                  are they slaked?

"I'm fifty years old. I have MS. They beat me up."
                                        he offers when
we insist he come order a sandwich with us
                                Subway counter
"Can I get a bag of chips, a drink?"
                                        his eye so neglected
I throw my arms around him, hug him, sisterly,
                                mujer at register begins to cry
We carry his order to table,
                        his legs fully turned in at knees, feet uncooperative
not even a shuffle to them, just laborious plow.

I plead with him to go to City Hall for help, for immediate need programs
                        "I don't know who to ask. I can't get around."

We eat. I send love through my skin, eyes, insisting.
        It's not enough, buy sandwich, give advice.
Late at night, I weep for him, for all of us who don't fit
        for vacuous disparity between beauty / pain.

    —all those nights spent under trestles when it was me that way—

He called while she was dying. Vista Cove, Santa Paula,
demanding her war widow's pension,

                                    said he needed boots,

more like boot up.

All we could think of was how he beat her, called her Dog.
                        Trampled her.

                                    She begged us to wire—
The courts had never allowed us
                        monetary control as her conservators
this one last time, we just pretended, bought her another day here.

In honor of the woman who loved children so much
                    she forced the city to put in a crosswalk
for grade school kids crossing, running late, between cars—
                    who might fall down   be hit—

Glen City Elementary, nearly thirty years later,
Remembered—   called
                    for family members to attend a play

little ones there now
so moved they chose the story to make their own homage
in tribute to a Santa Paula hero.

You went with your grandpa, brought me last lines,

So she could look out her window and see them safely cross
                    every day.

                    Something anyone might do—

                    Here in shadows, leaves
keep life close, fruit the taste of it, dusk, following plant

rows around crates, comfort here, home
                    nothing like a bed under stars
when we need.

Gleam now in rain slickening
                     arroyo willow branch
as blue elderberry summon
                         wind, Santa Anas
tangle reason, still leaves night
                    in bang by owl wing.

Here, hammocked over
                    oasis watering life,
rocks form mouths
                        predawn, calling.

Deep in night, corded sky ropes
                              tug through visceral root
harness reckoning, throttle
                      to timbre
thrum, strum, pluck gut sleeve
                          kindle fiddle full belly
flourish poppies as quarter notes
                      spiral double helix
high above California fan palm
                    until stars are born.

Joshua Trees of the first vandalized during
        shutdown, national park defunding

1,200 square miles at risk
        high desert, 45 might as well have burned it all
rangy succulent majesty
        said to straddle Mojave and Colorado Deserts,
incoming spray-painting rocks,
        smiley face, THE 419, three underscores
                felling Joshuas to make off-roading roads,
so they could drive into sensitive areas
            where vehicles are banned
by 2100 climate change rising temperatures
          may take it all, they're hurrying along.
People climbed the massive junipers to break
        branches for prohibited fires, it's welcome shade
        now gone.

"There is no Plan B for our national parks"—Rand Abbott

      "Donald Trump is literally destroying America."—Bill Prady

This morning, separating aloe pups, spider plant sprawl,
sage undergrowth, dried in drought. There she
          ran along, over stone circles laid for steps when wet.
      Today, so dry.
          At first, a quiver, then quicker, run, low, steady, mammal.
Golden, buff, fur—   endangered one in quiet refuge, this garden
Kangaroo
rat, related to beaver, pocket gopher
          running along, making room for me to thin, separate
her lodging space, cover, home—
          more hers than mine, endemic.

Yesterday, in Ventura County, a male gray wolf appeared,
          for first time in ninety-nine years, here.

Dazzled under luminosity
                        nitric acid photons airglow field
100 thousand million stars in the sky road milk   corn mush   acorn
take some home
                California, come home,
                          somewhere beyond brutal lies beauty,
unrequited,

requite now, quiet now, requite kindness,
                         mutual aid, reciprocal abundance, beauty
as far as land is poppied, Chaparral roam, bladderpod stand
                   let this dream, breath plume, vascular thrum
                   strengthen
stone tongues speaking in night as they shift along,
                  Playa sailing stones, wanderlusting
night unbroken, spirit unbroken,
                  drawing their lines in the sand

Your palms know where to go.

> What they imagine leads you.

Everything we muster moves us along,

like water mirroring itself remembers

> where to flow, how to go there.

In the dream you follow, in the dream we

fly over all of this direness   float   vaquitas.

We move like smallest porpoises, undulate in air, like swimming

> arms tight against our sides

California spread below us

> manzanitas gleaming in sun

stars ahead in darkness await our time there.

> For now, it is the offering we make.

Look at This Blue

Hidden Lake bluecurls   *from Hidden Lake, San Jacintos, Riverside*
County
                            on the shores of a single vernal pool, ephemeral
        trampling by hikers, sightseekers endangers
                each flower a hairy calyx with pointed sepals
                            tubular corona
                            fifty flowers might fit on a penny
                            a member of the mint family

                            delisting, seeds stored in seed bank
vulnerable

Will you take me as I am?

California

   —Joni Mitchell

Do the work:

Amah Mutsun Land Trust
Restoring Indigenous knowledge and practices
to Popeloutchom ancestral homelands
https://www.amahmutsunlandtrust.org

The Native American Land Conservancy's mission is to acquire,
preserve, and protect sacred lands in aboriginal territories of
Southern California.
http://nativeamericanland.org

Indian Land Tenure Foundation
https://iltf.org

NICWA
https://www.nicwa.org/about-icwa

CASA
https://casaforchildren.org

IRC
https://www.rescue.org/united-states/los-angeles-ca

Border Angels
https://www.borderangels.org

Justice in Motion
http://justiceinmotion.org

Kids in Need of Defense
https://supportkind.org

RAICES
https://www.raicestexas.org

Center for Empowering Refugees
https://www.cerieastbay.org

Intertribal Friendship House
https://www.ifhurbanrez.org

Southern California Indian Center
https://www.ocindiancenter.org

Ready California
https://www.caloes.ca.gov/ICESite/Pages/National-Preparedness
-Month.aspx

Californians for Pesticide Reform
https://www.pesticidereform.org

Deep Medicine Circle
http://www.deepmedicinecircle.org

Dr. Rupa Marya, One Earth
https://www.oneearth.org/contributor/dr-rupa-marya

Peninsula Open Space Trust
https://openspacetrust.org

Association of Ramaytush Ohlone (ARO)
https://www.ramaytush.org

Water Resource Center Archives
https://www.watereducation.org/california-environmental-
organizations-involved-water-issues

Cultural Conservancy
https://www.nativeland.org

Women's Earth Alliance
https://womensearthalliance.org

Sogorea Té Land Trust
https://sogoreate-landtrust.org

mak-'amham/Café Ohlone
https://www.makamham.com

Seventh Generation Fund
https://7genfund.org

Sovereign Bodies Institute
https://www.sovereign-bodies.org

Chris Remington, "Indigenous Communities and Environmental
Stewardship," CapRadio *California Native*
https://www.capradio.org/news/insight/2017/08/16/insight-081617b

Black Lives Matter Los Angeles
https://www.blmla.org

Immigrant Legal Resource Center
https://www.ilrc.org/who-we-are

California Farmworker Foundation
https://californiafarmworkers.org

California Asian Pacific Islander Legislative Caucus
https://apicaucus.legislature.ca.gov/community-resources

Asian Prisoner Support Committee
https://www.asianprisonersupport.com

Asian Pacific Environmental Network
https://apen4ej.org/who-is-apen

APIENC
https://apienc.org

California Partnership to End Domestic Violence
https://www.cpedv.org

Write Girl
https://www.writegirl.org

California Indian Studies & Scholars Association
http://www.californiaindianstudies.org

California Indian Law Association
https://www.calindianlaw.org

California Native Plant Society
https://www.cnps.org

Los Padres Forest Watch: Sespe Condor Sanctuary
https://lpfw.org/our-region/wildlife/california-condor

End Extinction San Diego
https://www.endextinctionsandiego.org

Afternotes:

*California Governor Gavin Newsom addressed the state's
homelessness crisis from the city of Sebastopol in Sonoma
County on Monday, where he signed a $12 billion bill for
homeless funding. . . . "Opportunity should not just be for some people."*

—KTVU

COVID-19 State Data Tracking
https://covid19.ca.gov/state-dashboard/#todays-update

Current California State Budget
http://www.ebudget.ca.gov

California Homelessness Tracking Site
https://www.bcsh.ca.gov/hcfc/hdis.html

California Endangered Species
https://wildlife.ca.gov/Conservation/CESA

Works Cited

Page xiii: Gillis, Tanya Tagaq. 2016. "Retribution." Track 2 on *Retribution*. Six Shooter Records, compact disc.

Page 6: Le Guin, Ursula K. "Concerning Ishi." The Ursula K. Le Guin Literary Trust. Accessed June 1, 2021. http://www.ursulakleguinarchive .com/Note-Ishi.html.

Page 6: Native Languages of the Americas. "Yana Indian Language (Yahi)." Accessed June 1, 2021. http://www.native-languages.org/yana.

Page 7: Cosgrove, Jaclyn, Alejandra Reyes-Velarde, and Alene Tchekmedyian. "'It's all going to burn': Man accused of setting Holy fire was a well-known troublemaker, neighbors say." *Los Angeles Times*, August 13, 2018. https://www.latimes.com/local/lanow/la-me-holy -firxe-arson-suspect-20180812-story.html.

Page 10: Jones, Jack, and Eric Malnic. "2 New Ojai Fires Erupt; Arson Seen: Body of Third Victim Discovered in Baldwin Hills." *Los Angeles Times*, July 4, 1985. https://www.latimes.com/archives/la-xpm-1985-07-04 -mn-9120-story.html.

Page 11: Palos Verdes/South Bay Audubon Society. "Blue Butterfly Project." Accessed June 1, 2021. https://pvsb-audubon.org/blue-butterfly -project.

Page 17: California Legislature. Senate. *Civil detention facilities: state investigation*. SB-622. California Legislature, 2019–2020 regular session. Introduced February 22, 2019.

Page 18: Pilkington, Ed, and Martin Pengelly. "'Let it be an arms race': Donald Trump appears to double down on nuclear expansion." *Guardian* (U.S. edition), December 24, 2016. https://www.theguardian .com/us-news/2016/dec/23/donald-trump-nuclear-weapons-arms -race.

Page 19: Badash, David. "Handcuffs, BB Guns Found in Home of 8 Year Old Boy Allegedly Tortured, Killed Because He Was Thought to Be Gay." New Civil Rights Movement. November 3, 2017. https://www.thenewcivilrightsmovement.com/2017/11/handcuffs_bb_guns_found_in_home_of_8_year_old_boy_tortured_killed_because_he_was_thought_to_be_gay.

Page 20: Pearce, Tim. "California's Largest Utility Could Face Murder Charges for Sparking Wildfires." *Daily Caller.* December 31, 2018. https://dailycaller.com/2018/12/31/pge-murder-manslaughter-california.

Page 20: Serna, Joseph, and Matt Hamilton. "PG&E Pleads Guilty to 84 Counts of Involuntary Manslaughter over Camp Fire." *Los Angeles Times,* March 23, 2020. https://www.latimes.com/california/story/2020-03-23/pge-pleads-guilty-to-84-counts-of-manslaughter-over-paradise-fire.

Page 33 (begins on): U.S. Fish & Wildlife Service. ECOS: Environmental Conservation Online System. Accessed June 1, 2021. https://ecos.fws.gov/ecp0/reports/ad-hoc-species-report?kingdom=V&kingdom=I&status=E&status=T&status=EmE&status=EmT&status=EXPE&status=EXPN&status=SAE&status=SAT&fcrithab=on&fstatus=on&fspecrule=on&finvpop=on&fgroup=on&header=Listed+Animals.

Page 44 (begins on): State of California Natural Resources Agency. *State and Federally Listed Endangered, Threatened, and Rare Plants of California.* April 2021. https://nrm.dfg.ca.gov/FileHandler.ashx?DocumentID=109390.

Pages 54–55: Amah Mutsun Tribal Band. "History." Accessed June 1, 2021. http://amahmutsun.org/history.

Page 56: Lindsay, Brendan C. *Murder State: California's Native American Genocide, 1846–1873.* Lincoln: University of Nebraska Press, 2012.

Page 56: Bell, Horace. *Reminiscences of a Ranger, Or, Early Times in Southern California.* Los Angeles: Yarnell, Caystile & Mathes, Printers, 1881.

Page 56: Wallace, William A., ed. "Indian Arrests." *Los Angeles Star,* December 3, 1853. USC Digital Library. http://digitallibrary.usc.edu /digital/collection/p15799coll68/id/1610.

Page 56: See also Meares, Hadley. "Genocide, Slavery, and L.A.'s Role in the Decimation of Native Californians." KCET. June 29, 2016. https:// www.kcet.org/shows/lost-la/genocide-slavery-and-l-a-s-role-in -the-decimation-of-native-californians.

Page 57: Blakemore, Erin. "The Enslaved Native Americans Who Made the Gold Rush Possible." History. A&E Television Networks. Updated August 31, 2018. https://www.history.com/news/the -enslaved-native-americans-who-made-the-gold-rush-possible.

Pages 57–58: Reséndez, Andrés. *The Other Slavery: The Uncovered Story of Indian Enslavement in America.* Boston: Houghton Mifflin Harcourt, 2016.

Page 58: Blakemore, Erin. "California's Little-Known Genocide." History. A&E Television Networks. Updated December 4, 2020. https://www .history.com/news/californias-little-known-genocide.

Page 63: Judicial Branch of California. "California Tribal Communities." California Courts. Updated 2021. https://www.courts.ca.gov/3066.htm.

Pages 63, 70: The Judicial Branch of California. "Jurisdiction in Indian Country." California Courts. Updated 2021. https://www.courts .ca.gov/8710.htm.

Pages 64–66: Hodge, Frederick Webb, ed. *Handbook of American Indians North of Mexico: Part I.* Smithsonian Institution, Bureau of American Ethnology. Washington, DC: Government Printing Office, 1907. https://digitalcommons.csumb.edu/cgi/viewcontent.cgi?article =1003&context=hornbeck_ind_3.

Pages 64–66: Wolf, Dan. "Chumash Tribe – Notes." *Keeper of Stories* (blog). February 27, 2012. http://keeperofstories.blogspot.com/2012/02/.

Pages 66–71: Magliari, Michael. "An American Genocide: The United States and the California Indian Catastrophe, 1846-1873." *Ethnohistory* 62, no. 2 (April 1, 2017): 341–342. https://doi.org/10.1215/00141801-3789465.

Pages 66–71: Akins, Damon, and William J. Bauer. *We Are the Land: A History of Native California*. Berkeley: University of California Press, 2021.

Pages 66–71: Wolf, Jessica. "Revealing the History of Genocide against California's Native Americans." Newsroom. UCLA. August 15, 2017. https://newsroom.ucla.edu/stories/revealing-the-history-of-genocide-against-californias-native-americans.

Pages 67–69: "California Genocide." Wikipedia. Updated May 25, 2021. https://en.wikipedia.org/wiki/California_genocide.

Pages 67–69: Madley, Benjamin. *An American Genocide: The United States and the California Indian Catastrophe, 1846-1873*. New Haven, CT: Yale University Press, 2017.

Pages 67–70: Glauner, Lindsay. "The Need for Accountability and Reparations: 1830-1976 the United States Government's Role in the Promotion, Implementation, and Execution of the Crime of Genocide against Native Americans." *DuPaul Law Review* 51, no. 3 (Spring 2002): 911–962. https://via.library.depaul.edu/cgi/viewcontent.cgi?article=1568&context=law-review.

Page 69: Susman, Amelia. "The Round Valley Indians of California: An Unpublished Chapter in *Acculturation in Seven (or Eight) American Indian Tribes*." *Contributions of the University of California Archaeological Research Facility*, 31 (1976)." https://digitalassets.lib.berkeley.edu/anthpubs/ucb/proof/pdfs/arf031-004.pdf.

Page 70: Dobuzinskis, Alex. "California Governor Apologizes to Native Americans, Cites 'Genocide'." Reuters. June 18, 2019. https://www.reuters .com/article/us-california-native-americans/california-governor -apologizes-to-native-americans-cites-genocide-idUSKCN1TK03P.

Page 70: California Legislature. Senate. *An act to add Division 6.5 (commencing with Section 8575) to the Public Resources Code, relating to the Gabrielino-Tongva Tribe.* SB-1134. January 31, 2008.

Page 70: Blakemore, Erin. "California Slaughtered 16,000 Native Americans. The State Finally Apologized for the Genocide." History. A&E Television Networks. June 19, 2019. https://www.history.com/news/native -american-genocide-california-apology.

Page 71: Chamings, Andrew. "The Golden Dragon Massacre: A Bloody Rampage in 1970s SF." SFGATE, June 15, 2021. https:// www.sfgate.com/sfhistory/article/golden-dragon-massacre-san -francisco-1977-16246542.php.

Page 71: Wallace, Kelly. "Forgotten Los Angeles History: The Chinese Massacre of 1871." Los Angeles Public Library. May 19, 2017. https://www .lapl.org/collections-resources/blogs/lapl/chinese-massacre-1871.

Page 71: Kesslen, Ben. "Gunman in 2018 Thousand Oaks Shooting Motivated by Hatred of College Students, Report Says." NBC News. July 1, 2021. https://www.nbcnews.com/news/us-news/gunman -2018-thousand-oaks-shooting-motivated-hatred-college-students -report-n1272936.

Page 71: Littlefield, Dana. "New Documentary Explores 1984 McDonald's Massacre in San Ysidro." *San Diego Union Tribune*, September 21, 2016. https://www.sandiegouniontribune.com/sd-me-mcdonalds -documentary-20160920-story.html.

Page 71: Johnson, Nikie. "San Bernardino Attack Timeline: Minutes of Terror, Years of Consequences." *San Bernardino Sun*, November 29, 2020. https://www.sbsun.com/2020/11/29/san-bernardino-attack -timeline-minutes-of-terror-years-of-consequences.

Page 71: Tsai, Joyce. "Memories on 50th Anniversary of Airplane Disaster in the East Bay Still Run Strong." *The Mercury News,* updated August 12, 2016. https://www.mercurynews.com/2014/05/06/memories-on-50th-anniversary-of-airplane-disaster-in-the-east-bay-still-run-strong.

Page 71: La Tour, Jesse. "The California Native American Genocide." *Fullerton Observer,* July 7, 2020. https://fullertonobserver.com/2020/07/07/the-california-native-american-genocide.

Page 73: Sacramento Fish & Wildlife Office. "Mission Blue Butterfly: Species Information." U.S. Fish & Wildlife Service. Updated December 1, 2017. https://www.fws.gov/sacramento/es_species/Accounts/Invertebrates/mission_blue_butterfly.

Page 74: McPhate, Mike. "California's black slaves and the myth of free soil." *California Sun,* January 23, 2019. https://www.californiasun.co/stories/californias-black-slaves-and-the-myth-of-free-soil.

Page 74: Fri, Robert. "Yana People to Receive Ishi's Brain." SFGATE, updated February 1, 2012. https://www.sfgate.com/opinion/openforum/article/Yana-People-To-Receive-Ishi-s-Brain-2931781.php.

Page 74: Southern Border Communities Coalition. "Deaths by Border Patrol Since 2010." Updated June 3, 2021. https://www.southernborder.org/deaths_by_border_patrol.

Pages 76–77: Ninan, Reena. "California Woman Valeria Alvarado Fatally Shot by Border Patrol Agent." ABC News. September 30, 2012. https://abcnews.go.com/US/valeria-alvarado-california-woman-fatally-shot-border-patrol/story?id=17359380.

Pages 76–77: U.S. Immigration and Customs Enforcement (ICE). "Detainee Death Report: SINGH, Simratpal." American Immigration Lawyers Association. Posted June 27, 2019. https://www.aila.org/File/Related/18121905f.pdf.

Pages 76–77: U.S. Immigration and Customs Enforcement (ICE). "Detainee Death Report: AMAR, Mergensana." American Immigration Lawyers Association. Posted June 27, 2019. https://www.aila.org/File/Related/18121905i.pdf.

Pages 76–77: U.S. Immigration and Customs Enforcement (ICE). "Detainee Death Report: RAMIREZ-ARREOLA, Augustina." American Immigration Lawyers Association. Accessed June 1, 2021. https://www.ice.gov/doclib/foia/reports/ddrRamirezArreolaAugustina.pdf

Pages 76–77, 82: U.S. Immigration and Customs Enforcement (ICE). "Detainee Death Report: TRAN, Huy Chi." American Immigration Lawyers Association. Posted December 19, 2018. https://www.aila.org/File/Related/18121905c.pdf.

Pages 76–77, 82: U.S. Immigration and Customs Enforcement (ICE). "Detainee Death Report: MIRIMANIAN, Gourgen." American Immigration Lawyers Association. Posted December 19, 2018. https://www.aila.org/File/Related/18121905.pdf.

Page 79: Adan, Melissa. "Family of Man Killed by Border Patrol Agent Says Non-Lethal Force Could've Saved His Life." CBS San Diego. Updated October 28, 2020. https://www.nbcsandiego.com/news/local/family-of-man-killed-by-border-patrol-agent-says-non-lethal-force-couldve-saved-his-life/2432195.

Page 82: McGreevy, Patrick. "California sues Trump over 'public charge' rule denying green cards to immigrants." *Los Angeles Times,* August 16, 2019. https://www.latimes.com/california/story/2019-08-16/california-immigration-lawsuit-trump-public-charge.

Page 85: Wiley, Hannah. "For 50th time, California sues the Trump administration — 'That's a lot of lawsuits.'" *Sacramento Bee,* May 13, 2019. https://www.sacbee.com/news/politics-government/capitol-alert/article230340579.html.

Page 85: Wolfe, Jan. "Trump sues California over tax return law." Reuters. August 6, 2019. https://www.reuters.com/article/us-usa -trump-california/trump-sues-california-over-tax-return-law -idUSKCN1UW22D.

Page 85: "Gov. Newsom Bashes Trump's Border Wall, Says California Won't 'Turn Its Back' On Asylum Seekers." CBS Los Angeles. March 11, 2019. https://losangeles.cbslocal.com/2019/03/11/newsom-interview -on-trump-border-wall.

Page 85: Stark, Kevin. "California sues Trump Administration over clean power rollback." KQED. August 13, 2019. https://www.kqed.org /science/1946454/california-sues-trump-administration-over-clean -power-rollback.

Pages 86–88: Garces, Audrey. "4 Bodies Recovered from Boat Fire off Santa Cruz Island." KQED. Updated September 2, 2019. https://www.kqed .org/news/11771713/boat-fire-off-southern-california-coast-leaves-34 -missing.

Pages 86, 88: Anderson, Erik. "How Ice a Half a World Away Affects Southern California Sea Levels." KPBS Public Media. June 17, 2019. https://www.kpbs.org/news/2019/jun/17/how-ice-half-world-away -affects-southern-california.

Page 91: History.com editors, "This Day in History: Marvin Gaye Is Shot and Killed by His Own Father." History. A&E Television Networks. Updated March 30,2021. https://www.history.com/this-day-in -history/marvin-gaye-is-shot-and-killed-by-his-own-father.

Page 95: Colón-Muñiz, Anaida and Magaly Lavadenz, eds. *Latino Civil Rights in Education.* New York: Routledge, 2016.

Page 95: Rasmussen, Cecilia. "Institute Tried to Drum 'Civilization' Into Indian Youth." *Los Angeles Times*, February 23, 2003. https://www .latimes.com/archives/la-xpm-2003-feb-23-me-then23-story.html.

Page 95: Sherman Indian Museum. "Sherman Indian High School Beginning to the Present." Accessed June 1, 2021. http://www.shermanindianmuseum.org/sherman_hist.htm.

Page 95: Sherman Indian Museum. "Sherman Cemetery." Accessed June 1, 2021. http://www.shermanindianmuseum.org.

Page 96: Smith, Stacey. "Pacific Bound: California's 1852 Fugitive Slave Law." Black Past. January 6, 2014. https://www.blackpast.org/african-american-history/pacific-bound-california-s-1852-fugitive-slave-law.

Page 96: Library of Congress. "Primary Documents in American History: Chinese Exclusion Act." Accessed June 1, 2021. https://www.loc.gov/rr/program/bib//ourdocs/chinese.html.

Page 97: California Legislature. Senate. *An act to add Chapter 8.5 (commencing with Section 8720) to Division 1 of Title 2 of the Government Code, relating to Mexican repatriation.* SB-760, chapter 663. October 7, 2005.

Page 99: United States Congress. *Restitution for World War II Internment of Japanese-Americans and Aleuts.* U.S. Code 50, chapter 52, section 4201. August 10, 1988.

Page 115: Upton, John (@johnupton). "During the shutdown, with Joshua Tree National Park open but no staff on duty, visitors cut down Joshua trees so they could drive into sensitive areas where vehicles are banned." Twitter. January 10, 2019. https://twitter.com/johnupton/status/1083387896403505153.

Page 115: Chiu, Allyson. "A travesty to this nation': People are destroying Joshua trees in Joshua Tree National Park." *Washington Post*, January 11, 2019. https://www.washingtonpost.com/nation/2019/01/11/travesty-this-nation-people-are-destroying-joshua-trees-joshua-tree-national-park.

Page 115: Prady, Bill (@billprady). "They cut down Joshua trees. In Joshua Tree National Park. Donald Trump is literally destroying America." Twitter. January 10, 2019. https://twitter.com/billprady /status/1083441963515269120?lang=en.

Page 120: Mitchell, Joni. 1971. "California." Track 6 on *Blue*. Reprise Records, vinyl.

Index

Coffee House Press began as a small letterpress operation in 1972 and has grown into an internationally renowned nonprofit publisher of literary fiction, essay, poetry, and other work that doesn't fit neatly into genre categories.

Coffee House is both a publisher and an arts organization. Through our *Books in Action* program and publications, we've become interdisciplinary collaborators and incubators for new work and audience experiences. Our vision for the future is one where a publisher is a catalyst and connector.

LITERATURE
is not the same thing as
PUBLISHING

Funder Acknowledgments

Coffee House Press is an internationally renowned independent book publisher and arts nonprofit based in Minneapolis, MN; through its literary publications and *Books in Action* program, Coffee House acts as a catalyst and connector—between authors and readers, ideas and resources, creativity and community, inspiration and action.

Coffee House Press books are made possible through the generous support of grants and donations from corporations, state and federal grant programs, family foundations, and the many individuals who believe in the transformational power of literature. This activity is made possible by the voters of Minnesota through a Minnesota State Arts Board Operating Support grant, thanks to the legislative appropriation from the Arts and Cultural Heritage Fund. Coffee House also receives major operating support from the Amazon Literary Partnership, Jerome Foundation, McKnight Foundation, Target Foundation, and the National Endowment for the Arts (NEA). To find out more about how NEA grants impact individuals and communities, visit www.arts.gov.

Coffee House Press receives additional support from Bookmobile; Dorsey & Whitney LLP; Elmer L. & Eleanor J. Andersen Foundation; Fredrikson & Byron, P.A.; the Matching Grant Program Fund of the Minneapolis Foundation; Mr. Pancks' Fund in memory of Graham Kimpton; the Schwab Charitable Fund; and the U.S. Bank Foundation.

The Publisher's Circle of Coffee House Press

Publisher's Circle members make significant contributions to Coffee House Press's annual giving campaign. Understanding that a strong financial base is necessary for the press to meet the challenges and opportunities that arise each year, this group plays a crucial part in the success of Coffee House's mission.

Recent Publisher's Circle members include many anonymous donors, Patricia A. Beithon, Anitra Budd, Andrew Brantingham, Dave & Kelli Cloutier, Mary Ebert & Paul Stembler, Jocelyn Hale & Glenn Miller, the Rehael Fund-Roger Hale/Nor Hall of the Minneapolis Foundation, Randy Hartten & Ron Lotz, Dylan Hicks & Nina Hale, William Hardacker, Kenneth & Susan Kahn, Stephen & Isabel Keating, the Kenneth Koch Literary Estate, Cinda Kornblum, Jennifer Kwon Dobbs & Stefan Liess, the Lambert Family Foundation, the Lenfestey Family Foundation, Sarah Lutman & Rob Rudolph, the Carol & Aaron Mack Charitable Fund of the Minneapolis Foundation, Gillian McCain, Malcolm S. McDermid & Katie Windle, Mary & Malcolm McDermid, Daniel N. Smith III & Maureen Millea Smith, Peter Nelson & Jennifer Swenson, Enrique & Jennifer Olivarez, Alan Polsky, Robin Preble, Jeffrey Sugerman & Sarah Schultz, Nan G. Swid, Grant Wood, and Margaret Wurtele.

For more information about the Publisher's Circle and other ways to support Coffee House Press books, authors, and activities, please visit www.coffeehousepress.org/pages/donate or contact us at info@coffeehousepress.org.

Allison Adelle Hedge Coke, a California Arts Council Legacy Artist, Fulbright scholar, First Jade Nurtured SiHui Female International Poetry Award recipient, recent Dan and Maggie Inouye Distinguished Chair in Democratic Ideals, and U.S. Library of Congress Witter Bynner fellow, has written seven books of poetry, one book of non-fiction, and a play. Following former fieldworker retraining in Santa Paula and Ventura in the mid-1980s, she began teaching, and she is now a distinguished professor of creative writing at the University of California, Riverside.

Look at This Blue was designed by
Bookmobile Design & Digital Publisher Services.
Text is set in Lora Regular.